The No-Point

MEDITERRANEAN COOKBOOK

Unlock Rapid Weight Loss with a 42-Day Meal Plan, Unlimited Flavorful Recipes, and an Essential Food List to Transform Your Lifestyle

Angelina P. Arias

CONTENTS

Introduction

Embracing the No-Point Mediterranean Lifestyle

Welcome to a transformative journey towards a healthier, happier you! My name is Angelina, and I've dedicated the past 15 years of my life to the world of nutrition and dietetics. As a seasoned dietitian, I've had the privilege of witnessing countless individuals achieve their weight loss goals and embrace a more vibrant lifestyle, all through the power of food.

Over the years, I've discovered that sustainable weight loss doesn't have to be synonymous with deprivation and restriction. Instead, it's about making mindful choices, savoring delicious foods, and building a balanced relationship with what we eat. The No-Point Mediterranean Lifestyle, which we will explore in this cookbook, is a testament to this philosophy.

This approach combines the time-tested wisdom of the Mediterranean diet with the liberating concept of "no-point" foods - those wholesome, nutrient-dense options that you can enjoy freely without counting calories or meticulously tracking portions. It's a lifestyle that celebrates abundance, flavor, and the sheer joy of eating.

In the pages that follow, you'll discover a treasure trove of delicious recipes, a comprehensive 42-day meal plan, and an essential food list to guide you every step of the way. You'll learn how to build a no-point pantry, calculate food and recipe points, and make mindful choices that support your weight loss goals.

Whether you're a seasoned cook or just starting your culinary journey, this cookbook is designed to empower you to take control of your health and well-being. Together, we will unlock the secrets to rapid, sustainable weight loss, all while savoring the vibrant flavors of the Mediterranean.

It's time to embrace a lifestyle that nourishes your body, delights your taste buds, and leaves you feeling energized and empowered. Let's embark on this exciting adventure together!

The Power of Unlimited Foods for Rapid Weight Loss

Imagine a world where you don't have to meticulously count every calorie or measure every portion. A world where you can savor delicious, satisfying meals without the guilt or anxiety that often accompanies traditional diets. That's the beauty of the No-Point Mediterranean Lifestyle.

By focusing on a wide array of wholesome, nutrient-dense foods that you can enjoy freely, this approach empowers you to break free from the cycle of restriction and deprivation. It shifts the focus from what you *can't* have to what you *can* have – an abundance of flavorful, nourishing options that support your weight loss journey.

The science behind this approach is clear: when you prioritize whole, unprocessed foods, your body naturally feels more satisfied and less inclined to overeat. You'll experience sustained energy levels, improved digestion, and a renewed sense of vitality.

Your Journey to a Healthier, Happier You

This cookbook is more than just a collection of recipes; it's a roadmap to a healthier, happier you. It's about embracing a lifestyle that nourishes your body, mind, and soul.

As you embark on this journey, you'll discover the power of mindful eating, the importance of physical activity, and the joy of savoring every bite. You'll learn to navigate social situations and dining out with confidence, and you'll develop strategies for staying motivated and on track.

Remember, weight loss is not just about shedding pounds; it's about transforming your relationship with food and cultivating a deep sense of self-love and well-being.

This cookbook is your companion on this transformative journey. It's filled with practical tips, inspiring stories, and delicious recipes that will make your weight loss journey a joyful and sustainable one.

So, let's turn the page and begin this exciting adventure together. Your healthier, happier self awaits!

Chapter 1: Understanding the No-Point Mediterranean Diet

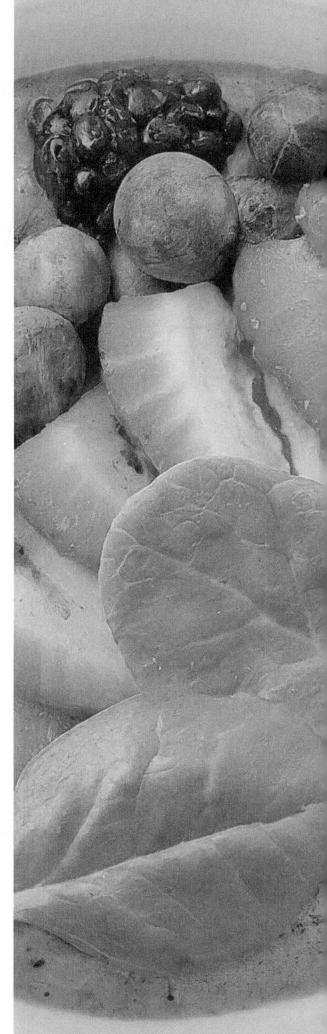

Key Principles of the No-Point Approach

The No-Point approach is a revolutionary way to think about weight loss that emphasizes freedom, abundance, and nourishment. It's a philosophy that prioritizes whole, unprocessed foods, allowing you to enjoy a wide variety of delicious and satisfying options without the burden of calorie counting or point tracking.

Here are the key principles that underpin this empowering approach:

1. **Embrace Unlimited Foods:** At the heart of the No-Point approach is the concept of "unlimited foods." These are nutrient-dense, minimally processed options that you can enjoy freely without worrying about portion sizes or points. These foods form the foundation of a healthy diet and provide your body with the essential vitamins, minerals, and fiber it needs to thrive.

2. **Prioritize Plant-Based Foods:** The No-Point approach encourages a predominantly plant-based diet, rich in fruits, vegetables, whole grains, legumes, nuts, and seeds. These foods are packed with antioxidants, fiber, and other beneficial nutrients that support weight loss, improve overall health, and reduce the risk of chronic diseases.

3. **Include Lean Protein and Healthy Fats:** While the emphasis is on plant-based foods, the No-Point approach also includes moderate amounts of lean protein and healthy fats. Fish, seafood, poultry, eggs, yogurt, and cheese are all excellent sources of protein, while extra virgin olive oil, avocados, and nuts provide heart-healthy fats.

4. **Limit Processed Foods and Added Sugars:** The No-Point approach discourages the consumption of highly processed foods, refined carbohydrates, and added sugars. These foods are often high in calories, low in nutrients, and can contribute to weight gain and other health problems.

5. **Practice Mindful Eating:** Mindful eating is a crucial component of the No-Point approach. It involves paying attention to your hunger cues, savoring each bite, and eating without distractions. By cultivating a mindful approach to eating, you can develop a healthier relationship with food and make more conscious choices that support your weight loss goals.

6. **Enjoy Regular Physical Activity:** While the No-Point approach focuses on food, it also recognizes the importance of regular physical activity. Exercise not only helps burn calories but also improves overall health, boosts mood, and reduces stress.

7. **Embrace a Holistic Lifestyle:** The No-Point approach is more than just a diet; it's a holistic lifestyle that encompasses all aspects of your well-being. It encourages you to prioritize sleep, stress management, and self-care, all of which play a crucial role in achieving and maintaining a healthy weight.

By embracing these key principles, you'll embark on a transformative journey towards a healthier, happier you. The No-Point approach is not about deprivation or restriction; it's about celebrating abundance, nourishing your body, and finding joy in the simple act of eating.

The Mediterranean Diet: A Foundation for Success

The Mediterranean diet has long been celebrated as a beacon of health and longevity. Rooted in the traditional eating patterns of countries bordering the Mediterranean Sea, this dietary approach emphasizes whole, unprocessed foods, a vibrant array of fruits and vegetables, and an abundance of heart-healthy fats. It's a way of eating that nourishes both body and soul, fostering a sense of well-being that extends far beyond the plate.

So, why is the Mediterranean diet such a perfect partner for the No-Point approach?

Firstly, both philosophies prioritize **whole, plant-based foods**. The Mediterranean diet champions fruits, vegetables, legumes, whole grains, and nuts – all of which are cornerstones of the No-Point approach's "unlimited foods" list. This synergy makes it incredibly easy to create delicious, satisfying meals that support your weight loss goals without sacrificing flavor or variety.

Secondly, both approaches recognize the importance of **healthy fats**. The Mediterranean diet is renowned for its inclusion of extra virgin olive oil, olives, avocados, and nuts – all rich sources of monounsaturated and polyunsaturated fats that promote heart health, reduce inflammation, and support satiety. In the No-Point approach, these healthy fats play a key role in keeping you feeling full and satisfied, preventing cravings and overeating.

Thirdly, both the Mediterranean diet and the No-Point approach emphasize **moderation and balance**. They encourage you to savor a wide variety of foods in appropriate portions, fostering a healthy relationship with food that is both sustainable and enjoyable.

In my experience as a dietitian, I've seen firsthand the transformative power of the Mediterranean diet. I've worked with countless clients who have successfully lost weight, improved their health markers, and embraced a more vibrant lifestyle by incorporating the principles of this dietary approach. I recall one client, Sarah, who struggled with yo-yo dieting and felt trapped in a cycle of restriction and deprivation. When we transitioned her to a Mediterranean-style eating pattern, focusing on No-Point foods, she experienced a newfound sense of freedom and joy in her relationship with food. She lost weight steadily and sustainably, and more importantly, she felt energized, empowered, and in control of her health.

By marrying the No-Point approach with the wisdom of the Mediterranean diet, this cookbook offers a unique and powerful path to rapid weight loss and lasting well-being. It's a testament to the fact that healthy eating can be both delicious and liberating, and that sustainable weight loss is achievable without sacrificing the pleasures of the table.

The Science Behind Rapid Weight Loss

The No-Point Mediterranean approach isn't just a fad diet; it's backed by a solid foundation of scientific evidence. Research has shown that diets rich in whole, plant-based foods and low in processed foods and added sugars can lead to significant weight loss and improve overall health.

- **Increased Satiety:** Studies have shown that diets rich in fiber, protein, and healthy fats lead to greater feelings of fullness and satisfaction, reducing the likelihood of overeating and snacking. The No-Point approach's emphasis on unlimited fruits, vegetables, legumes, and lean protein ensures you'll feel satisfied and nourished throughout the day.
- **Improved Metabolic Health:** Research suggests that a diet rich in whole foods can improve insulin sensitivity and metabolic health, making it easier for your body to burn fat and regulate blood sugar levels. The No-Point approach's focus on minimally processed foods and limited added sugars helps support healthy metabolism and weight loss.
- **Reduced Inflammation:** Chronic inflammation is linked to a variety of health problems, including obesity, heart disease, and diabetes. The Mediterranean diet, with its abundance of antioxidants and anti-inflammatory compounds, has been shown to reduce inflammation and promote overall health.
- **Sustainable Weight Loss:** Unlike restrictive diets that often lead to yo-yo dieting and weight regain, the No-Point Mediterranean approach promotes sustainable weight loss by focusing on long-term lifestyle changes. By embracing a balanced and enjoyable way of eating, you're more likely to stick with it and achieve lasting results.

Busting Common Diet Myths

Let's address some common misconceptions about weight loss and healthy eating:

1. **Myth 1: All Calories are Created Equal:** Not all calories are the same. The quality of your food choices matters just as much as the quantity. 100 calories from a handful of almonds will nourish your body differently than 100 calories from a processed snack. The No-Point approach prioritizes nutrient-dense foods that fuel your body and support your weight loss goals.
2. **Myth 2: Carbs are the Enemy:** Carbohydrates are an essential source of energy for your body. The key is to choose complex carbohydrates found in whole grains, fruits, and vegetables over refined carbohydrates found in processed foods. The No-Point approach includes plenty of healthy carbs to keep you energized and satisfied.
3. **Myth 3: Fat Makes You Fat:** Healthy fats are crucial for overall health and can actually aid in weight loss. They promote satiety, support hormone balance, and help your body absorb essential nutrients. The No-Point approach includes plenty of healthy fats from sources like extra virgin olive oil, avocados, and nuts.
4. **Myth 4: You Need to Starve Yourself to Lose Weight:** Deprivation and restriction are not sustainable approaches to weight loss. The No-Point approach encourages you to eat until you're comfortably full, focusing on nourishing foods that keep you satisfied and prevent cravings.
5. **Myth 5: Rapid Weight Loss is Unhealthy:** While extreme weight loss methods can be detrimental, a well-planned, balanced approach like the No-Point Mediterranean diet can lead to safe and effective weight loss. By prioritizing whole foods and incorporating regular physical activity, you can achieve your goals without compromising your health.

The No-Point Mediterranean Diet: A Safe and Effective Approach

The No-Point Mediterranean diet is a safe and sustainable approach to weight loss that prioritizes your overall health and well-being. By focusing on nutrient-dense, minimally processed foods, you'll provide your body with the fuel it needs to thrive while shedding excess pounds. This approach is not about deprivation or restriction; it's about embracing a balanced and enjoyable way of eating that supports your weight loss goals and sets you up for long-term success.

Chapter 2: Mini-Course on Food Lists and Point Calculation

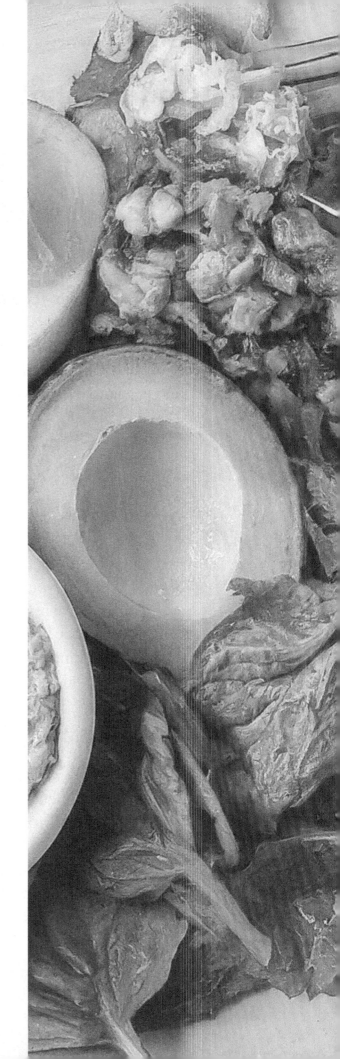

Understanding the Essential Food List

The cornerstone of the No-Point Mediterranean approach is the Essential Food List. This carefully curated collection of foods serves as your guide to building a healthy, balanced, and satisfying diet that supports your weight loss goals. By focusing on these nutrient-dense options, you'll nourish your body, fuel your energy levels, and promote overall well-being.

The Essential Food List

The Essential Food List is divided into several categories:

1. **Vegetables:** This category includes a wide array of colorful and flavorful vegetables, both starchy and non-starchy. Think leafy greens, cruciferous vegetables, root vegetables, and everything in between. Aim to include a variety of vegetables in your meals and snacks to ensure you're getting a broad spectrum of nutrients.

2. **Fruits:** From juicy berries to tropical delights, fruits add natural sweetness and a wealth of vitamins, minerals, and antioxidants to your diet. Enjoy them fresh, frozen, or dried, but be mindful of added sugars in canned or processed varieties.

3. **Whole Grains:** Opt for whole grains over refined grains whenever possible. Whole-wheat bread, brown rice, quinoa, oats, and barley are excellent choices. These foods provide sustained energy, fiber, and essential nutrients.

4. **Legumes:** Beans, lentils, chickpeas, and peas are packed with protein, fiber, and iron. They're a versatile and affordable addition to your pantry and can be used in a variety of dishes, from salads and soups to stews and dips.

5. **Nuts and Seeds:** Almonds, walnuts, cashews, sunflower seeds, and pumpkin seeds are excellent sources of healthy fats, protein, and fiber. Enjoy them in moderation as a snack, or add them to yogurt, salads, or oatmeal for a boost of nutrients.

6. **Lean Protein:** Fish, seafood, poultry, eggs, yogurt, and cheese provide essential protein for building and repairing tissues. Choose lean cuts of meat and poultry, and opt for low-fat or non-fat dairy products.

7. **Healthy Fats:** Extra virgin olive oil, olives, avocados, and avocado oil are rich in heart-healthy monounsaturated and polyunsaturated fats. These fats promote satiety, support healthy cholesterol levels, and reduce inflammation.

8. **Herbs and Spices:** Flavor your dishes with a variety of herbs and spices instead of relying on salt or added sugars. Herbs and spices add depth and complexity to your meals while providing additional health benefits.

Embracing Abundance

The beauty of the Essential Food List is that it encourages you to embrace abundance rather than restriction. You can enjoy unlimited quantities of most of these foods, allowing you to feel satisfied and nourished without worrying about counting calories or tracking points.

By prioritizing these wholesome, minimally processed options, you'll naturally gravitate towards a healthier, more balanced way of eating. Your body will thank you with increased energy, improved digestion, and sustainable weight loss.

Remember, the Essential Food List is your guide, not a rigid set of rules. Experiment with different foods, flavors, and combinations to discover what works best for you. Embrace the joy of cooking and eating, and let the No-Point Mediterranean approach nourish your body and soul.

How to Calculate Food Points

While the No-Point Mediterranean approach encourages you to focus on enjoying unlimited quantities of wholesome foods, it's still helpful to understand the underlying nutritional principles that guide food choices. This understanding will empower you to make informed decisions even when faced with foods that aren't on the Essential Food List.

Simplified Calculation Methods

Remember, we're not using any trademarked point systems here. Instead, we'll focus on understanding the nutritional value of foods and how they contribute to your weight loss goals.

- **The Macro Ratio Method:** This method involves looking at the balance of macronutrients - protein, carbohydrates, and fats - in a food. Generally, foods higher in protein and fiber and lower in refined carbohydrates and unhealthy fats are considered more favorable for weight loss.

Method 1: The Macro Ratio Method with Custom Point Calculation

Understanding the Macro Ratio

The macro ratio method simplifies food choices by focusing on the balance of macronutrients in your diet. Macronutrients are the three primary building blocks of food: protein, carbohydrates, and fats. Each macronutrient plays a vital role in your body, providing energy, supporting growth and repair, and regulating various bodily functions.

In the context of weight loss, the macro ratio method suggests prioritizing foods that are:

- **Higher in protein:** Protein helps build and maintain muscle mass, which is crucial for boosting metabolism and burning more calories at rest. It also promotes satiety, keeping you feeling full and satisfied.
- **Higher in fiber:** Fiber is a type of carbohydrate that your body can't digest. It adds bulk to your diet, promoting fullness and aiding digestion. Fiber also helps regulate blood sugar levels, preventing spikes and crashes that can lead to cravings and overeating.
- **Lower in refined carbohydrates:** Refined carbohydrates, such as white bread, pastries, and sugary drinks, are quickly digested and can cause blood sugar spikes and crashes. These fluctuations can lead to increased hunger and cravings, making it harder to stick to your weight loss goals.
- **Lower in unhealthy fats:** Unhealthy fats, such as saturated and trans fats, can contribute to weight gain, heart disease, and other health problems. The macro ratio method encourages you to choose foods with healthy fats, such as those found in olive oil, avocados, and nuts.

Simplifying the Calculation

You don't need to be a math whiz to use the macro ratio method. Simply pay attention to the nutrition label on packaged foods or use a reliable food database to find the macronutrient breakdown of your favorite foods. Aim for a balance that emphasizes protein and fiber while limiting refined carbohydrates and unhealthy fats.

A common starting point for a weight-loss macro ratio is:

- **Protein: 30%**
- **Carbohydrates: 40%**
- **Fats: 30%**

How to Calculate

1. **Determine your daily calorie target.** This will depend on your individual needs and goals. Consult a dietitian or use an online calculator to estimate your daily calorie needs for weight loss.
2. **Calculate grams for each macro.**
   Protein: Multiply your daily calorie target by 0.3 (30%) and divide by 4 (calories per gram of protein).
   Carbohydrates: Multiply your daily calorie target by 0.4 (40%) and divide by 4 (calories per gram of carbohydrate).

Fats: Multiply your daily calorie target by 0.3 (30%) and divide by 9 (calories per gram of fat).

Example:

Let's say your daily calorie target for weight loss is 1500 calories.

- **Protein:** (1500 x 0.3) / 4 = 112.5 grams of protein per day
- **Carbohydrates:** (1500 x 0.4) / 4 = 150 grams of carbohydrates per day
- **Fats:** (1500 x 0.3) / 9 = 50 grams of fat per day

Now, when you're choosing foods, aim to stay within these macro targets. Prioritize foods that are naturally high in protein and fiber and low in refined carbs and unhealthy fats.

Custom Point Calculation

To further simplify the decision-making process, we can assign custom points to foods based on their macro ratios and overall nutritional value. Here's a basic framework:

- **Protein:** 1 point per 10 grams
- **Fiber:** -1 point per 5 grams (subtract from the total)
- **Refined Carbohydrates:** 1 point per 10 grams
- **Unhealthy Fats:** 2 points per 5 grams

How to Calculate

1. **Determine the macronutrient breakdown of the food.** Use the nutrition label or a reliable food database.
2. **Calculate points for each macro.**
   - **Protein Points:** Divide the grams of protein by 10.
   - **Fiber Points:** Divide the grams of fiber by 5 and subtract this number from the total.
   - **Refined Carbohydrate Points:** Divide the grams of refined carbohydrates by 10.
   - **Unhealthy Fat Points:** Divide the grams of unhealthy fats by 5 and multiply by 2
3. **Add the points for each macro to get the total food points.**

Example:

Let's calculate the custom points for a serving of grilled salmon with roasted vegetables.

- **Salmon (3 oz):**
    Protein: 22 grams / 10 = 2.2 points
    Fiber: 0 grams / 5 = 0 points
    Refined Carbs: 0 grams / 10 = 0 points
    Unhealthy Fats: Let's assume 2 grams / 5 x 2 = 0.8 points
    Total Points for Salmon: 2.2 + 0 + 0 + 0.8 = 3 points
- **Roasted Vegetables (1 cup):**
    Protein: Let's assume 3 grams / 10 = 0.3 points
    Fiber: Let's assume 5 grams / 5 = 1 point (subtract from the total)
    Refined Carbs: Let's assume 10 grams / 10 = 1 point
    Unhealthy Fats: 0 grams / 5 x 2 = 0 points
    Total Points for Vegetables: 0.3 - 1 + 1 + 0 = 0.3 points
- **Total Meal Points:** 3 + 0.3 = 3.3 points

Interpreting the Points

- **0-2 points:** Excellent choice for weight loss, prioritize these foods
- **3-5 points:** Moderate choice, enjoy in moderation
- **6+ points:** Limit these foods or consider healthier alternatives

Remember: This custom point system is a simplified tool to guide your food choices. It's essential to prioritize overall nutritional value and listen to your body's hunger and fullness cues.

Why is the Macro Ratio Method with Custom Point Calculation Effective?

This combined approach offers several benefits:

1. **Simplicity:** It provides a clear and easy-to-understand way to evaluate food choices.
2. **Flexibility:** You can adjust the point system to fit your individual needs and preferences.
3. **Mindful Eating:** It encourages you to be more aware of the nutritional value of your food choices.
4. **Supports Weight Loss:** By prioritizing nutrient-dense, low-point foods, you'll create a calorie deficit and promote healthy weight loss.

Pros and Cons

Pros:

- Simple and easy to use
- Customizable to fit your needs
- Promotes mindful eating
- Supports weight loss

Cons:

- May not be as accurate as a professionally developed point system
- Requires some initial effort to calculate points for your favorite foods

By incorporating the macro ratio method with custom point calculation, you have a powerful tool to navigate your food choices and support your weight loss journey. Remember, it's about progress, not perfection. Embrace the flexibility of the No-Point Mediterranean approach, and enjoy the journey to a healthier, happier you!

The Nutrient Density Method: This method focuses on the overall nutritional value of a food. Foods rich in vitamins, minerals, and antioxidants are considered more nutrient-dense and thus more beneficial for your health and weight loss journey.

Method 2: The Nutrient Density Method with Custom Point Calculation

Understanding Nutrient Density

The nutrient density method focuses on the overall nutritional value of a food, considering the amount of vitamins, minerals, antioxidants, and other beneficial compounds it provides relative to its calorie content. Foods that are high in nutrients and relatively low in calories are considered more nutrient-dense, making them valuable allies in your weight loss journey.

Custom Point Calculation

To simplify food choices using the nutrient density approach, we can again implement a custom point system. Here's a basic framework:

- **Vitamins and Minerals:** -1 point per significant source (e.g., Vitamin C, Iron, Calcium)
- **Antioxidants:** -1 point per significant source (e.g., Polyphenols, Flavonoids)
- **Fiber:** -1 point per 5 grams
- **Calories:** 1 point per 100 calories

How to Calculate

1. **Identify the key nutrients in the food.** Use the nutrition label or a reliable food database.
2. **Calculate points for each nutrient category.**
   Vitamins and Minerals Points: Count the number of significant vitamins and minerals present and subtract that number from the total.
   Antioxidant Points: Count the number of significant antioxidants present and subtract that number from the total
   Fiber Points: Divide the grams of fiber by 5 and subtract this number from the total.
   Calorie Points: Divide the total calories by 100.
3. **Add the points for each category to get the total food points.**

Example:

Let's calculate the custom points for a serving of Greek yogurt with berries.

1. **Greek Yogurt (1 cup):**
   Vitamins and Minerals: Let's assume it has significant amounts of Calcium and Vitamin D = -2 points
   Antioxidants: Negligible = 0 points
   Protein: Let's assume 20 grams / 10 = 2 points
   Fiber: 0 grams / 5 = 0 points
   Calories: Let's assume 150 calories / 100 = 1.5 points
   Total Points for Greek Yogurt: -2 + 0 + 2 + 0 + 1.5 = 1.5 points

2. **Berries (½ cup):**
   Vitamins and Minerals: Let's assume it has a significant amount of Vitamin C = -1 point
   Antioxidants: Let's assume significant antioxidants are present = -1 point
   Protein: Negligible = 0 points
   Fiber: Let's assume 4 grams / 5 = 0.8 points (subtract from total)
   Calories: Let's assume 50 calories / 100 = 0.5 points
   Total Points for Berries: -1 -1 + 0 - 0.8 + 0.5 = -1.3 points

3. **Total Meal Points:** 1.5 - 1.3 = 0.2 points

Interpreting the Points

- **Negative points or 0-2 points:** Excellent choice for weight loss, prioritize these foods.
- **3-5 points:** Moderate choice, enjoy in moderation.
- **6+ points:** Limit these foods or consider healthier alternatives.

●

Why is the Nutrient Density Method with Custom Point Calculation Effective?

This approach emphasizes the nutritional quality of food, encouraging you to choose options that provide a wealth of vitamins, minerals, and antioxidants while keeping calories in check. It supports:

- **Optimal Health:** Prioritizing nutrient-dense foods ensures your body gets the essential nutrients it needs to function optimally and thrive.
- **Satiety:** Foods rich in fiber and protein promote fullness and help prevent overeating
- **Weight Loss:** By focusing on lower-calorie, nutrient-rich options, you can create a calorie deficit and support healthy weight loss.
- **Disease Prevention:** A diet rich in vitamins, minerals, and antioxidants can help reduce the risk of chronic diseases.

Things to Watch Out For

- **Don't Rely Solely on Points:** While the point system is a helpful guide, it's essential to consider the overall balance and variety in your diet.
- **Beware of "Health Halo" Foods:** Some foods may seem healthy but are high in calories or added sugars. Always read the nutrition label carefully.
- **Listen to Your Body:** Pay attention to your hunger and fullness cues, and adjust your food choices accordingly.

Embrace the Power of Nutrient Density

The nutrient density method with custom point calculation empowers you to make informed choices that prioritize both health and weight loss. By focusing on foods that nourish your body and support your goals, you'll create a sustainable and enjoyable eating pattern that sets you up for long-term success. Remember, it's a journey, not a race. Embrace the process, savor the flavors, and celebrate every step towards a healthier, happier you!

The Glycemic Index Method: This method considers how quickly a food raises your blood sugar levels. Foods with a lower glycemic index (GI) are digested more slowly, leading to a more gradual increase in blood sugar and sustained energy levels.

Method 3: The Glycemic Index (GI) Method with Custom Point Calculation

Understanding the Glycemic Index

The Glycemic Index (GI) is a ranking system that measures how quickly a carbohydrate-containing food raises your blood sugar levels. Foods are assigned a GI value on a scale of 0 to 100, with higher values indicating a faster rise in blood sugar.

In the context of weight loss, the GI method suggests prioritizing foods with a lower GI. These foods are digested more slowly, leading to a more gradual increase in blood sugar and sustained energy levels. This can help prevent blood sugar spikes and crashes, which can trigger cravings, overeating, and fat storage.

Custom Point Calculation

To incorporate the GI method into your food choices, we can use a custom point system that considers both the GI value and the amount of carbohydrates in a food. Here's a basic framework:

- **Low GI Foods (GI 0-55):** 0 points per serving
- **Medium GI Foods (GI 56-69):** 1 point per serving
- **High GI Foods (GI 70-100):** 2 points per serving

How to Calculate

1. **Find the GI value of the food.** Use a reliable GI database or look for the GI value on the food packaging.
2. **Determine the serving size and the amount of carbohydrates per serving.** Use the nutrition label or a food database.
3. **Assign points based on the GI value and serving size.**
   Low GI foods: 0 points
   Medium GI foods: 1 point
   High GI foods: 2 points

Example:

Let's calculate the custom points for a serving of brown rice and a serving of white bread.

- **Brown Rice (cooked, ½ cup):**
    GI value: 50 (Low GI)
    Carbohydrates per serving: 22 grams
    Total Points: 0 points
- **White Bread (1 slice):**
    GI value: 70 (High GI)
    Carbohydrates per serving: 15 grams
    Total Points: 2 points

Interpreting the Points

- **0 points:** Excellent choice for weight loss, prioritize these foods.
- **1-2 points:** Moderate choice, enjoy in moderation, especially when combined with protein and healthy fats.
- **3+ points:** Limit these foods or consider healthier alternatives.

Why is the Glycemic Index Method with Custom Point Calculation Effective?

This approach helps you:

- **Stabilize blood sugar levels:** By choosing low GI foods, you'll prevent blood sugar spikes and crashes, leading to more stable energy levels and reduced cravings.
- **Promote satiety:** Low GI foods are often higher in fiber, which promotes fullness and helps you feel satisfied longer.
- **Support weight loss:** By managing blood sugar levels and promoting satiety, you're less likely to overeat and more likely to achieve your weight loss goals.
- **Improve overall health:** Stable blood sugar levels are associated with a reduced risk of type 2 diabetes, heart disease, and other chronic conditions.

Things to Watch Out For

- **GI Value is Not the Only Factor:** Consider the overall nutritional value of the food, including its fiber, protein, and fat content.
- **Processing Can Affect GI:** The way a food is prepared or processed can affect its GI value. For example, mashed potatoes have a higher GI than boiled potatoes.
- **Individual Variations:** The GI value of a food can vary slightly from person to person. Pay attention to how different foods affect your blood sugar levels.

Embrace the Power of the Glycemic Index

The Glycemic Index method with custom point calculation offers a valuable tool for managing blood sugar levels, promoting satiety, and supporting your weight loss journey. By incorporating more low GI foods into your diet and being mindful of portion sizes, you can create a sustainable and enjoyable eating pattern that nourishes your body and helps you achieve your goals. Remember, it's about making informed choices and finding a balance that works for you.

The Best Method for the No-Point Diet: A Holistic Approach

While each of the methods discussed offers valuable insights into food choices, the most effective approach for the No-Point Mediterranean diet is a holistic one that combines all three. This allows you to make informed decisions based on a comprehensive understanding of a food's nutritional value, macronutrient balance, and impact on blood sugar levels.

By considering the macro ratios, nutrient density, and glycemic index of your food choices, you'll create a balanced and satisfying diet that supports your weight loss goals and promotes overall health. Remember, the No-Point approach is about freedom and abundance, not restriction. It's about enjoying a wide variety of wholesome, delicious foods that nourish your body and soul.

Practically Determining the GI of a Food (Not Recipes)

While calculating the exact GI value of a complex recipe requires laboratory testing, there are practical ways to estimate the GI of individual foods to guide your choices.

1. **Reference a GI Database:** Several reliable online databases provide GI values for a wide variety of foods. Search for the specific food item you're interested in and note its GI value.
2. **Look for the GI Symbol:** Some packaged foods may carry the GI Symbol, indicating that the product has been tested and certified as having a low GI.
3. **General Guidelines:** Keep these general principles in mind:
   - **Whole, unprocessed foods tend to have a lower GI:** Fruits, vegetables, legumes, and whole grains generally have a lower GI than refined carbohydrates like white bread, pastries, and sugary drinks.
   - **Cooking methods can affect GI:** The way a food is prepared can influence its GI. For example, al dente pasta has a lower GI than overcooked pasta.

➢ **Fiber content matters:** Foods high in fiber tend to have a lower GI because fiber slows down digestion and absorption.

➢ **Fat and protein can lower GI:** Combining carbohydrates with protein or fat can help slow down the absorption of glucose, leading to a lower GI for the meal.

4. **Observe Your Body's Response:** Pay attention to how different foods affect your energy levels and hunger cues. If you notice a significant spike and crash in energy after eating a particular food, it may have a higher GI.

Remember:

- **Focus on the Big Picture:** Don't get too caught up in calculating the exact GI of every food. Prioritize whole, unprocessed foods from the Essential Food List and use the GI as a general guideline.
- **Combine Foods Strategically:** Pair higher GI foods with protein and healthy fats to slow down their absorption and reduce their impact on blood sugar levels.
- **Listen to Your Body:** Pay attention to how different foods make you feel and *adjust your choices accordingly.*

By using these practical strategies and focusing on the overall nutritional value of your food choices, you'll be well-equipped to make informed decisions that support your weight loss journey and promote long-term health. The No-Point Mediterranean approach is about flexibility and enjoyment, so don't be afraid to experiment and discover what works best for you.

Why Some Foods Are Considered "No-Point"

Foods on the Essential Food List are generally considered "no-point" because they are:

- **Nutrient-Dense:** They are packed with vitamins, minerals, and antioxidants that support your overall health and well-being.
- **High in Fiber:** Fiber promotes satiety, regulates digestion, and helps stabilize blood sugar levels.
- **Low in Calories:** Many of these foods are naturally low in calories, allowing you to eat larger portions without exceeding your daily energy needs.
- **Minimally Processed:** They are close to their natural state, free from added sugars, unhealthy fats, and artificial ingredients.

Points to Watch Out For

While enjoying the freedom of the No-Point approach, it's important to be mindful of certain foods that can hinder your weight loss progress:

1. **Highly Processed Foods:** These foods are often high in calories, unhealthy fats, added sugars, and sodium, and offer little nutritional value.
2. **Refined Carbohydrates:** White bread, pastries, and sugary drinks can cause blood sugar spikes and crashes, leading to cravings and overeating.
3. **Sugary Drinks:** Sodas, fruit juices, and sweetened teas are loaded with empty calories and can contribute to weight gain.
4. **Excessive Amounts of Added Fats:** While healthy fats are important, be mindful of portion sizes, especially when it comes to oils and nuts, as they are calorie-dense.

Illustrative Examples

1. **A handful of almonds vs. a packaged granola bar:** While both may have a similar calorie count, the almonds are a more favorable choice due to their higher protein and fiber content and lack of added sugars.
2. **A bowl of oatmeal with berries vs. a bowl of sugary cereal:** The oatmeal with berries is a better option as it has a lower glycemic index, providing sustained energy and keeping you feeling full longer.
3. **Grilled salmon with roasted vegetables vs. fried chicken with french fries:** The salmon and vegetables offer lean protein, healthy fats, and plenty of nutrients, while the fried chicken and fries are high in unhealthy fats and refined carbohydrates.

Mediterranean Food Nutritional Table

Food	Serving Size	Calories	Protein (g)	Carbs (g)	Fiber (g)	Fat (g)
Spinach (cooked)	1 cup	41	5	7	4	0.4
Salmon (grilled)	3 oz	175	22	0	0	10
Chickpeas (cooked)	½ cup	140	8	24	6	2
Brown Rice (cooked)	½ cup	108	2	22	1.5	1
Extra Virgin Olive Oil	1 tbsp	119	0	0	0	14
Avocado (½ medium)	-	160	2	9	7	15

Essential Mediterranean Foods for the No-Point Diet

The following table showcases key Mediterranean foods and their nutritional information, categorized based on their typical point value in a No-Point diet.

Legend:

- **NP:** No-Point Foods (enjoy freely)
- **LP:** Low-Point Foods (enjoy in moderation)
- **GI:** Glycemic Index

Vegetables (NP)

Food	Serving Size	Calories	Protein (g)	Carbs (g)	Fiber (g)	Fat (g)	GI	Points
Spinach (cooked)	1 cup	41	5	7	4	0.4	Low	NP
Broccoli (steamed)	1 cup	55	4	11	5	0.5	Low	NP
Bell Peppers (raw)	1 medium	30	1	7	2	0	Low	NP
Tomatoes (raw)	1 medium	22	1	5	1	0	Low	NP
Kale (cooked)	1 cup	36	3	7	3	0.5	Low	NP

Fruits (NP)

Food	Serving Size	Calories	Protein (g)	Carbs (g)	Fiber (g)	Fat (g)	GI	Points
Berries (mixed)	1 cup	62	1	14	4	0.5	Low	NP
Apple (medium)	1	95	0	25	4	0	Low	NP
Grapes	1 cup	104	1	27	1	0	Low-Medium	NP
Orange (medium)	1	62	1	15	3	0	Low	NP

Whole Grains (NP/LP)

Food	Serving Size	Calories	Protein (g)	Carbs (g)	Fiber (g)	Fat (g)	GI	Points
Brown Rice (cooked)	½ cup	108	2	22	1.5	1	Medium	NP/LP
Quinoa (cooked)	½ cup	111	4	20	2.5	2	Low	NP
Whole Wheat Bread	1 slice	80	4	15	2	1	Medium	LP

Legumes (NP)

Food	Serving Size	Calories	Protein (g)	Carbs (g)	Fiber (g)	Fat (g)	GI	Points
Chickpeas (cooked)	½ cup	140	8	24	6	2	Low	NP
Lentils (cooked)	½ cup	115	9	20	8	0.5	Low	NP
Black Beans (cooked)	½ cup	114	8	20	6	1	Low	NP

Lean Protein (NP/LP)

Food	Serving Size	Calories	Protein (g)	Carbs (g)	Fiber (g)	Fat (g)	GI	Points
Salmon (grilled)	3 oz	175	22	0	0	10	Low	NP
Chicken Breast (grilled, skinless)	3 oz	140	26	0	0	3	-	NP
Eggs	1 large	70	6	0	0	5	-	NP
Greek Yogurt (plain, non-fat)	1 cup	100	17	6	0	0	Low	NP
Feta Cheese (crumbled)	¼ cup	100	6	4	0	8	-	LP

Healthy Fats (LP)

Food	Serving Size	Calories	Protein (g)	Carbs (g)	Fiber (g)	Fat (g)	GI	Points
Extra Virgin Olive Oil	1 tbsp	119	0	0	0	14	-	LP
Avocado	½ medium	160	2	9	7	15	Low	LP
Olives	10 large	40	0	1	1	4	-	LP
Almonds	¼ cup	207	7	8	4	18	-	LP

Zero-Point Foods in this Context

Based on the No-Point principles and the above table, here are some examples of foods you can generally enjoy freely:

- Most Vegetables: Spinach, broccoli, bell peppers, tomatoes, kale, etc.
- Most Fruits: Berries, apples, oranges, etc.
- Legumes: Chickpeas, lentils, black beans.
- Lean Protein: Salmon, chicken breast, eggs, plain non-fat Greek yogurt

Remember: Even with "no-point" foods, portion control and mindful eating are still key to successful weight loss. Listen to your body's hunger and fullness cues, and enjoy these foods as part of a balanced and varied diet.

Exploring Further

This is just a glimpse into the vast array of delicious and nutritious Mediterranean foods you can incorporate into your No-Point journey. As you progress through the cookbook, you'll discover countless more options to tantalize your taste buds and support your weight loss goals.

How to Calculate Recipe Points

hile the No-Point Mediterranean approach encourages you to focus on enjoying unlimited quantities of wholesome, single-ingredient foods, you'll inevitably encounter recipes that combine multiple ingredients, some of which might not be on the "no-point" list. In these cases, it's helpful to have a method for estimating the overall point value of a recipe to guide your portion control and ensure you're staying on track with your weight loss goals.

Simplified Calculation Method

We'll continue to use the custom point system we established earlier, based on macronutrient ratios, nutrient density, and glycemic index. Here's the basic framework:

- **Protein:** 1 point per 10 grams
- **Fiber:** -1 point per 5 grams (subtract from the total)
- **Refined Carbohydrates:** 1 point per 10 grams
- **Unhealthy Fats:** 2 points per 5 grams
- **Low GI Foods:** 0 points per serving
- **Medium GI Foods:** 1 point per serving
- **High GI Foods:** 2 points per serving

How to Calculate

1. **Gather Nutritional Information:**
   - For each ingredient in the recipe, find its nutritional breakdown (calories, protein, carbs, fiber, fat) using a food label, reliable database, or online resources.
   - Note the GI value of any significant carbohydrate sources in the recipe.
2. **Calculate Points for Each Ingredient:**
   - Use the custom point system outlined above to calculate the points for each ingredient based on its macro ratios, nutrient density, and GI value.
   - Multiply the points per serving by the number of servings of that ingredient used in the recipe to get the total points for that ingredient.
3. **Add Up the Points:**
   - Sum the points for all ingredients to get the total recipe points.
4. **Divide by Servings:**
   - Divide the total recipe points by the number of servings the recipe yields to get the points per serving.

Example:

Let's calculate the points for a simple Mediterranean salad recipe:

Ingredients:
- 2 cups mixed greens (NP)
- ½ cup chopped cucumber (NP)
- ½ cup cherry tomatoes (NP)
- ¼ cup crumbled feta cheese (1 point per serving)
- 2 tablespoons olive oil (2 points per serving)
- 1 tablespoon balsamic vinegar (0 points)

Calculation:
- Mixed greens, cucumber, tomatoes: 0 points (No-Point vegetables)
- Feta cheese: 1 point
- Olive oil: 2 points
- Balsamic vinegar: 0 points
- Total Recipe Points: 0 + 0 + 0 + 1 + 2 + 0 = 3 points
- Servings: Let's assume this recipe makes 2 servings
- Points per Serving: 3 / 2 = 1.5 points

Example: Mediterranean Salad Point Calculation

Let's break down the point calculation for the Mediterranean Salad example using the template:

Ingredient	Serving Size	Calories	Protein	Carbs	Fiber	Fat	GI	Points per Serving	Servings Used	Total Points
Mixed Greens	2 cups	16	1	3	2	0	Low	0	1	0
Cucumber (chopped)	½ cup	8	0.5	2	0.5	0	Low	0	1	0
Cherry Tomatoes	½ cup	15	1	3	1	0	Low	0	1	0
Feta Cheese (crumbled)	¼ cup	100	6	4	0	8	-	1	1	1
Olive Oil	2 tablespoons	238	0	0	0	28	-	2	1	2
Balsamic Vinegar	1 tablespoon	14	0	3	0	0	-	0	1	0
Total		383	8.5	15	3.5	28				3
Points per Serving									2	1.5

Explanation

1. We estimated the nutritional values for the mixed greens, cucumber, and cherry tomatoes based on typical values for these vegetables.
2. The feta cheese and olive oil were assigned points based on the provided information (1 point per serving for feta, 2 points per serving for olive oil).
3. Balsamic vinegar is considered a "no-point" food due to its low calorie and negligible macro content.
4. The total points for the recipe were calculated by adding the points for each ingredient.
5. Finally, the total points were divided by the number of servings (2) to get the points per serving (1.5).

This example demonstrates how you can use the template to calculate the points for any recipe. Remember to adjust the serving sizes and nutritional information based on the specific ingredients and quantities used in your recipe.

By understanding how to calculate recipe points, you can make informed choices about portion sizes and ensure that your meals align with your weight loss goals while still enjoying the delicious flavors of the Mediterranean diet.

Tips for Estimating Points When Dining Out

- **Focus on the Essential Food List:** Choose dishes that are centered around No-Point foods like vegetables, fruits, lean protein, and whole grains.
- **Be Mindful of Sauces and Dressings:** These can often be high in added sugars and unhealthy fats. Ask for dressings on the side or choose lighter options like vinaigrette.
- **Watch Portion Sizes:** Even with No-Point foods, be mindful of portion sizes to avoid overeating.
- **Don't Be Afraid to Ask Questions:** Ask your server about the ingredients and preparation methods of dishes to make informed choices.

Embrace Flexibility

Remember, this point calculation method is a tool to guide your choices, not a rigid rule. The No-Point Mediterranean approach is about flexibility and enjoying a variety of wholesome foods. Use this method as a helpful reference, but don't let it become a source of stress or anxiety. Focus on nourishing your body, listening to your hunger cues, and savoring the flavors of the Mediterranean.

Chapter 3: Building Your No-Point Pantry

Essential Foods for Your Kitchen

Creating a well-stocked pantry is crucial for embracing the No-Point Mediterranean lifestyle. By having a variety of nutritious and flavorful ingredients on hand, you'll be well-equipped to whip up delicious and satisfying meals without the need for constant trips to the grocery store. Let's explore the essential foods that will form the foundation of your No-Point pantry.

Mediterranean Zero-Point Staples

These foods should be the stars of your pantry, as they can be enjoyed freely and form the basis of countless delicious and nourishing meals:

1. **Fresh Vegetables:** Stock up on a colorful array of vegetables, including leafy greens (spinach, kale, romaine lettuce), cruciferous vegetables (broccoli, cauliflower, Brussels sprouts), root vegetables (carrots, sweet potatoes, beets), and other favorites like bell peppers, cucumbers, tomatoes, onions, and garlic.
2. **Fresh Fruits:** Choose a variety of fruits based on your preferences and what's in season. Apples, bananas, oranges, berries, grapes, pears, and melons are all excellent choices. Consider buying some frozen fruits for smoothies or quick desserts.
3. **Whole Grains:** Keep a selection of whole grains on hand, such as brown rice, quinoa, oats, barley, and whole-wheat couscous. These versatile ingredients can be used in salads, side dishes, and main courses.
4. **Legumes:** Dried or canned beans, lentils, and chickpeas are pantry powerhouses. They're packed with protein, fiber, and iron, and can be used in soups, stews, salads, and dips.
5. **Nuts and Seeds:** Almonds, walnuts, cashews, sunflower seeds, and pumpkin seeds provide healthy fats, protein, and fiber. Keep a variety on hand for snacking or adding to yogurt, salads, or oatmeal.

6. **Lean Protein:** Stock up on canned tuna, salmon, or sardines packed in water or olive oil for quick and easy protein sources. Consider keeping frozen chicken breasts or fish fillets on hand for easy meal preparation.
7. **Healthy Fats:** Extra virgin olive oil is a must-have for cooking and dressings. Also consider keeping avocados on hand for salads, sandwiches, or dips.
8. **Herbs and Spices:** A well-stocked spice rack is essential for adding flavor and depth to your dishes. Some key Mediterranean herbs and spices to include are basil, oregano, rosemary, thyme, garlic powder, onion powder, paprika, and cumin.

Additional Mediterranean Pantry Staples

While not necessarily "no-point" foods, these additional items are frequently used in Mediterranean cuisine and can add variety and flavor to your meals:

1. **Whole Wheat Pasta and Bread:** Choose whole-wheat varieties over refined options for added fiber and nutrients.
2. **Vinegars:** Balsamic vinegar, red wine vinegar, and apple cider vinegar are great for salad dressings and marinades.
3. **Canned Tomatoes:** Diced tomatoes, crushed tomatoes, and tomato paste are essential for sauces, soups, and stews.
4. **Broths and Stocks:** Vegetable broth or chicken stock can be used as a base for soups, stews, and risotto.
5. **Dried Fruits:** Dates, figs, and apricots can be enjoyed as a snack or added to oatmeal or yogurt for sweetness.

Building a Sustainable Pantry

Remember, the key to a successful No-Point pantry is to focus on whole, unprocessed foods that you enjoy and that fit your lifestyle. Start with the essentials and gradually add new items as you explore different recipes and flavors. Don't be afraid to experiment and get creative in the kitchen! By stocking your pantry with nutritious and delicious ingredients, you'll be well on your way to embracing the No-Point Mediterranean lifestyle and achieving your weight loss goals.

Fresh fruits and vegetables are the cornerstone of the No-Point Mediterranean diet. They provide essential vitamins, minerals, antioxidants, and fiber that support your overall health and weight loss goals. Make it a priority to keep your refrigerator and fruit bowl stocked with a colorful variety of fresh produce.

Here are some tips for stocking up on fresh produce:

1. **Shop Seasonally:** Choose fruits and vegetables that are in season for optimal flavor and freshness. Visit your local farmer's market or check your grocery store's seasonal produce section.
2. **Choose a Variety of Colors:** The different colors of fruits and vegetables represent different phytonutrients, so aim for a rainbow of colors in your shopping cart.
3. **Plan Ahead:** Make a list of the fruits and vegetables you'll need for the week and stick to it. This will help prevent impulse buys and ensure you have everything you need for your meals and snacks.
4. **Store Properly:** Learn the best ways to store different types of produce to maximize their freshness and shelf life. Some fruits and vegetables, like berries and leafy greens, are best stored in the refrigerator, while others, like tomatoes and avocados, can be kept on the counter until ripe.
5. **Prep Ahead:** Wash and chop vegetables ahead of time to make it easier to incorporate them into your meals throughout the week.
6. **Don't Forget Frozen:** Frozen fruits and vegetables can be a convenient and affordable option, especially when fresh produce is out of season. Choose varieties without added sugars or sauces.

Pantry Staples for Quick and Easy Meals

In addition to fresh produce, certain pantry staples can make it easier to whip up quick and healthy meals on busy days. Here are some essentials to keep on hand:

1. **Canned Beans and Lentils:** These provide a quick and easy source of protein and fiber. Choose low-sodium or no-salt-added varieties.
2. **Whole Grain Pasta and Bread:** Keep a box of whole-wheat pasta or a loaf of whole-grain bread in your pantry for quick and satisfying meals.

3. **Nuts and Nut Butters:** Almonds, walnuts, cashews, and natural nut butters like almond butter or peanut butter make for convenient and nutritious snacks or additions to meals.
4. **Canned Tuna or Salmon:** Opt for tuna or salmon packed in water or olive oil for a quick and easy protein source.
5. **Extra Virgin Olive Oil:** This heart-healthy oil is essential for cooking, dressings, and marinades.
6. **Vinegars:** Balsamic vinegar, red wine vinegar, and apple cider vinegar add flavor and depth to dishes.
7. **Herbs and Spices:** Experiment with different herbs and spices to create flavorful meals without relying on added salt or sugar.
8. **Whole Grain Crackers or Rice Cakes:** These can be topped with avocado, hummus, or nut butter for a quick and satisfying snack.
9. **Oatmeal:** Steel-cut or rolled oats make for a hearty and nutritious breakfast option.

By stocking your pantry with these essential foods, you'll be well-prepared to create delicious and satisfying No-Point Mediterranean meals that support your weight loss goals and nourish your body from the inside out. Remember, a well-stocked pantry is a key ingredient for success on your journey to a healthier, happier you!

Navigating the Grocery Store with Confidence

Grocery shopping can be overwhelming, especially when trying to adopt a new eating pattern like the No-Point Mediterranean diet. However, with a little planning and knowledge, you can confidently navigate the aisles and fill your cart with nourishing and delicious foods that support your weight loss goals.

Before You Go

1. **Make a List:** Plan your meals for the week and create a shopping list based on the recipes you'll be making. This will help you stay focused and avoid impulse buys.
2. **Check Your Pantry:** Take inventory of what you already have on hand to avoid unnecessary purchases.
3. **Eat a Snack:** Don't go grocery shopping on an empty stomach, as this can lead to unhealthy cravings and impulse buys.

At the Grocery Store

1. **Stick to the Perimeter:** Most whole, unprocessed foods, like fruits, vegetables, lean protein, and dairy, are found around the perimeter of the grocery store. Focus your shopping efforts in these areas.
2. **Read Labels Carefully:** Pay close attention to nutrition labels, especially when buying packaged foods. Look for items with minimal ingredients, low added sugar and sodium content, and healthy fats.
3. **Choose Whole Grains:** When buying bread, pasta, or cereal, opt for whole-grain varieties over refined options.
4. **Explore the Bulk Section:** The bulk section can be a great place to find nuts, seeds, dried fruits, and whole grains at a lower cost.
5. **Don't Be Afraid to Ask:** If you're unsure about a product or its ingredients, don't hesitate to ask a store employee for assistance.

Tips for Smart Shopping

- **Shop on a Full Stomach:** As mentioned earlier, avoid shopping when you're hungry to prevent impulsive decisions.
- **Bring Your Own Bags:** Reusable bags are not only eco-friendly but can also help you stay organized and avoid impulse buys at the checkout line.
- **Shop Alone:** If possible, shop alone to avoid distractions and stay focused on your list.
- **Avoid the Center Aisles:** The center aisles are typically filled with processed foods and sugary drinks. Limit your time in these areas.
- **Compare Prices:** Don't be afraid to compare prices and choose the most affordable options.

Navigating the No-Point Way

When choosing foods for your No-Point Mediterranean diet, keep these tips in mind:

1. **Prioritize Fresh Produce:** Fill your cart with a colorful variety of fruits and vegetables. These should form the foundation of your meals and snacks.
2. **Choose Lean Protein:** Opt for fish, seafood, poultry, eggs, and legumes as your primary protein sources.
3. **Embrace Healthy Fats:** Include avocados, olives, nuts, seeds, and extra virgin olive oil in your diet.

4. **Limit Processed Foods:** Avoid packaged foods with long ingredient lists, added sugars, and unhealthy fats.
5. **Read Labels Carefully:** Pay attention to serving sizes and nutritional information to make informed choices.

By following these tips and focusing on the Essential Food List, you can navigate the grocery store with confidence and stock your pantry with the foods you need to succeed on your No-Point Mediterranean journey. Remember, grocery shopping is an opportunity to make choices that support your health and well-being. Embrace the process and enjoy the journey to a healthier, happier you!

Chapter 4:

No-Point Recipes for Every Occasion

1. Sunshine Scramble

This vibrant scramble is a fantastic way to kick-start your day with a burst of colors and nutrients. The egg whites offer a lean protein source, while the spinach, bell peppers, and tomatoes contribute essential vitamins, minerals, and antioxidants. It's a light and satisfying breakfast that will keep you energized without weighing you down.

Prep Time: 5 minutes **Cook Time**: 5 minutes **Total Time**: 10 minutes **Servings**: 1

Ingredients:

- 3 egg whites
- ½ cup chopped spinach
- ¼ cup chopped bell peppers
- ¼ cup chopped tomatoes
- Pinch of oregano and basil
- Salt and pepper to taste

Alternative ingredients for low budget and allergies:

- If bell peppers are unavailable or cause allergies, substitute with an equal amount of chopped zucchini or mushrooms.

Directions:

1. Heat a non-stick pan over medium heat.
2. Add the chopped spinach, bell peppers, and tomatoes to the pan. Sauté until softened, about 3-4 minutes.
3. In a separate bowl, whisk the egg whites with a fork until frothy. Season with salt and pepper.

4. Pour the egg whites into the pan with the vegetables. Scramble gently until cooked through, about 2-3 minutes.
5. Sprinkle with oregano and basil.
6. Serve immediately.

Nutritional facts:

- **Macronutrients:**
    Calories: ~100
    Protein: ~18g
    Carbs: ~8g
    Fat: ~1g
- **Micronutrients:**
    Vitamin D: negligible
    Calcium: ~50mg
    Iron: ~2mg
    Potassium: ~300mg

Special diet specification and recommendation:

- Suitable for vegetarian and gluten-free diets.
- For a vegan version, substitute the egg whites with a plant-based scramble alternative like tofu scramble.

Chef tips to make it healthier and cook faster:

- Prep the vegetables the night before to save time in the morning.
- Add a pinch of red pepper flakes for a touch of spice.
- Serve with a side of whole-wheat toast or a piece of fruit for a more filling breakfast.

Recipe Points: 0 points (all ingredients are from the no-point food list)

Ingredient	Serving Size	Calories	Protein	Carbs	Fiber	Fat	GI	Points per Serving	Servings Used	Total Points
Egg whites	3	51	12	0	0	0	-	0	1	0
Spinach (cooked)	½ cup	20.5	2.5	3.5	2	0.2	Low	0	1	0
Bell Peppers (raw)	¼ cup	7.5	0.25	1.75	0.5	0	Low	0	1	0
Tomatoes (raw)	¼ cup	5.5	0.25	1.25	0.25	0	Low	0	1	0
Oregano and Basil	Pinch	~0	~0	~0	~0	~0	-	0	-	0
Salt and Pepper	To taste	~0	~0	~0	~0	~0	-	0	-	0
Total		~84.5	~15	~6.5	~2.75	~0.2				0
Points per Serving									1	0

2. Mediterranean Oatmeal

A warm and comforting bowl of oatmeal is a classic breakfast staple, and this Mediterranean twist adds a burst of flavor and antioxidants. The rolled oats provide sustained energy and fiber, while the berries and walnuts add sweetness, crunch, and heart-healthy fats. Cinnamon adds a touch of warmth and spice, making this a truly satisfying and nourishing way to start your day.

Prep Time: 5 minutes **Cook Time**: 5-7 minutes **Total Time**: 10-12 minutes **Servings**: 1

Ingredients:

- ½ cup rolled oats
- 1 cup unsweetened almond milk or water
- ½ cup mixed berries
- 1 tablespoon chopped walnuts
- Sprinkle of cinnamon

Alternative ingredients for low budget and allergies:

- If you don't have almond milk, you can use water or any other unsweetened plant-based milk.
- For nut allergies, substitute the walnuts with an equal amount of pumpkin seeds or sunflower seeds.

Directions:

1. In a saucepan, combine the oats and almond milk (or water).
2. Bring to a boil over medium heat, then reduce heat to low and simmer for 5-7 minutes, or until the oats are cooked and the mixture has thickened.
3. Stir in the mixed berries.
4. Top with chopped walnuts and a sprinkle of cinnamon.
5. Serve warm and enjoy!

Nutritional facts:

Macronutrients:
    Calories: ~300
    Protein: ~10g
    Carbs: ~50g
    Fiber: ~8g
    Fat: ~10g
Micronutrients:
    Vitamin D: negligible
    Calcium: ~100mg (if using fortified almond milk)
    Iron: ~3mg
    Potassium: ~350mg

Special diet specification and recommendation:

- Suitable for vegetarian and gluten-free diets.
- For a vegan version, ensure the granola used is also vegan.

Chef tips to make it healthier and cook faster:

- Soak the oats overnight in the almond milk or water for quicker cooking in the morning.
- Add a pinch of ground flaxseed for extra omega-3 fatty acids.
- If you prefer a sweeter oatmeal, drizzle with a small amount of honey or maple syrup (consider points if using).

Recipe Points: 0 points (all ingredients are from the no-point food list, except for the optional honey/maple syrup)

Ingredient	Serving Size	Calories	Protein	Carbs	Fiber	Fat	GI	Points per Serving	Servings Used	Total Points
Rolled Oats	½ cup	150	5	27	4	3	Low	0	1	0
Unsweetened Almond Milk	1 cup	30	1	1	0	2.5	-	0	1	0
Mixed Berries	½ cup	31	0.5	7	2	0.25	Low	0	1	0
Walnuts (chopped)	1 tablespoon	45	1	2	1	4	-	0	1	0
Cinnamon	Sprinkle	~0	~0	~0	~0	~0	-	0	-	0
Total		~256	~7.5	~37	~7	~9.75				0
Points per Serving									1	0

3. Greek Yogurt Parfait

This parfait is a delightful combination of creamy Greek yogurt, sweet berries, and crunchy granola, offering a perfect balance of protein, carbohydrates, and healthy fats. It's a quick and easy breakfast or snack that will keep you feeling full and satisfied throughout the morning.

Prep Time: *5 minutes* **Cook Time:** *None* **Total Time:** *5 minutes* **Servings:** *1*

Ingredients:

- 1 cup plain non-fat Greek yogurt
- ½ cup sliced strawberries
- ¼ cup granola (ensure it's made with zero-point ingredients like oats, nuts, and seeds)
- Drizzle of honey (optional, consider points)

Alternative ingredients for low budget and allergies:

- If strawberries are not in season or too expensive, you can use any other type of berries or chopped fruit like peaches or apples.
- For those with nut allergies, ensure the granola is nut-free or substitute it with a mixture of oats, seeds, and dried fruit.

Directions:

1. In a glass or bowl, layer the Greek yogurt, sliced strawberries, and granola.
2. Repeat the layers until the glass or bowl is filled, ending with a layer of granola.
3. If desired, drizzle with a small amount of honey.
4. Enjoy immediately.

Nutritional facts:

Macronutrients:

Calories: ~250 (without honey)

Protein: ~20g

Carbs: ~30g

Fiber: ~5g

Fat: ~5g

Micronutrients:

Vitamin D: negligible (unless yogurt is fortified)

Calcium: ~200mg

Iron: ~1mg

Potassium: ~400mg

Special diet specification and recommendation:

- Suitable for vegetarian diets.
- For a vegan version, use a plant-based yogurt alternative and ensure the granola is also vegan.

Chef tips to make it healthier and faster:

- Prepare the parfait in individual jars or containers the night before for a grab-and-go breakfast.
- Add a sprinkle of chia seeds or flaxseed for extra fiber and omega-3 fatty acids
- If you want to add more protein, consider adding a scoop of protein powder to the yogurt.

Recipe Points: 0 points (without honey, all ingredients are from the no-point food list)

Ingredient	Serving Size	Calories	Protein	Carbs	Fiber	Fat	GI	Points per Serving	Servings Used	Total Points
Plain non-fat Greek Yogurt	1 cup	100	17	6	0	0	Low	0	1	0
Strawberries (sliced)	½ cup	23	0.5	6	1.5	0.2	Low	0	1	0
Granola (zero-point)	¼ cup	~120	~3	~20	~3	~4	Medium	0	1	0
Honey (optional)	Drizzle	~20	0	5	0	0	-	~0.5	-	0
Total		~243 (without honey)	~20.5	~31	~4.5	~4.2				0 (without honey)
Points per Serving									1	0 (without honey)

4. Savory Chickpea Scramble

This hearty and flavorful scramble is a fantastic plant-based alternative to traditional scrambled eggs. Chickpeas provide a good source of protein and fiber, while the spinach adds vitamins and minerals. The combination of cumin and paprika creates a warm and inviting aroma, making this a satisfying and nutritious breakfast or brunch option.

Prep Time: 5 minutes **Cook Time:** 10 minutes **Total Time:** 15 minutes **Servings:** 2

Ingredients:

- 1 cup cooked chickpeas, mashed
- ½ cup chopped spinach
- ¼ cup chopped onion
- 1 tablespoon olive oil
- Pinch of cumin and paprika
- Salt and pepper to taste

Alternative ingredients for low budget and allergies:

- If you don't have fresh spinach, you can use frozen spinach, thawed and squeezed dry.
- For those avoiding oil, you can sauté the onion in a bit of water or vegetable broth instead.

Directions:

1. Heat the olive oil in a large skillet over medium heat.
2. Add the chopped onion and sauté until softened and translucent, about 5 minutes.
3. Add the mashed chickpeas and spinach to the skillet. Cook, stirring occasionally, until the spinach is wilted and the chickpeas are heated through, about 5 minutes.
4. Season with cumin, paprika, salt, and pepper to taste.
5. Serve warm with a side of whole-wheat toast or a dollop of plain yogurt.

Macronutrients:

      Calories: ~200

      Protein: ~10g

      Carbs: ~30g

      Fiber: ~7g

      Fat: ~5g

Micronutrients:

      Vitamin D: negligible

      Calcium: ~50mg

      Iron: ~3mg

      Potassium: ~300mg

Special diet specification and recommendation:

- Suitable for vegan and gluten-free diets
- A great option for those looking for a high-protein, plant-based breakfast.

Chef tips to make it healthier and cook faster:

- Cook a large batch of chickpeas ahead of time to have on hand for quick meals throughout the week.
- Add a squeeze of lemon juice for a touch of brightness.
- Top with chopped fresh herbs like parsley or cilantro for extra flavor and nutrients

Ingredient	Serving Size	Calories	Protein	Carbs	Fiber	Fat	GI	Points per Serving	Servings Used	Total Points
Chickpeas (cooked)	1 cup	280	16	48	12	4	Low	0	1	0
Spinach (cooked)	½ cup	20.5	2.5	3.5	2	0.2	Low	0	1	0
Onion (chopped)	¼ cup	15	0.3	3.5	0.4	0	-	0	1	0
Olive Oil	1 tablespoon	120	0	0	0	14	-	1.2	1	1.2
Cumin & Paprika	Pinch	~0	~0	~0	~0	~0	-	0	-	0
Salt and Pepper	To taste	~0	~0	~0	~0	~0	-	0	-	0
Total		~435.5	~18.8	~55	~14.4	~14.2				1.2
Points per Serving									2	0.6

5. Tuna Salad Stuffed Tomatoes:

These stuffed tomatoes offer a refreshing and light lunch option, packed with protein and healthy fats. The tuna provides omega-3 fatty acids, while the vegetables add vitamins, minerals, and fiber. The Greek yogurt adds creaminess without extra fat, and the fresh dill provides a bright, herbaceous flavor.

Prep Time: *10 minutes* **Cook Time**: *None* **Total Time**: *10 minutes* **Servings**: 2

Ingredients:

- 2 large tomatoes
- 1 can tuna in water, drained
- ¼ cup chopped celery
- 2 tablespoons plain non-fat Greek yogurt
- 1 tablespoon chopped fresh dill
- Salt and pepper to taste

Alternative ingredients for low budget and allergies:

- If fresh dill is not available, you can use dried dill or substitute with another fresh herb like parsley or chives
- If you have a shellfish allergy, substitute the tuna with canned salmon or cooked chickpeas.

Directions:

1. Cut the tops off the tomatoes and use a spoon to scoop out the insides, creating a hollow space.
2. In a bowl, combine the tuna, chopped celery, Greek yogurt, and dill.
3. Season with salt and pepper to taste.
4. Fill the hollowed-out tomatoes with the tuna salad mixture.
5. Serve chilled or at room temperature.

Nutritional facts (per serving):

Macronutrients:

      Calories: ~150

      Protein: ~20g

      Carbs: ~10g

      Fiber: ~2g

      Fat: ~5g

Micronutrients:

      Vitamin D: negligible

      Calcium: ~50mg

      Iron: ~1mg

      Potassium: ~300mg

Special diet specification and recommendation:

- Suitable for gluten-free and dairy-free diets (if using dairy-free yogurt).
- A great option for a light and refreshing lunch or snack.

Chef tips to make it healthier and faster:

- Use a small melon baller to scoop out the tomato insides for a neater presentation.
- Add a pinch of red pepper flakes for a touch of spice.
- Serve with a side salad or whole-grain crackers for a more complete meal

Recipe Points: 0 points (all ingredients are from the no-point food list)

Ingredient	Serving Size	Calories	Protein	Carbs	Fiber	Fat	GI	Points per Serving	Servings Used	Total Points
Tomatoes	2 large	45	2	10	2	0	Low	0	1	0
Tuna in water (drained)	1 can (5 oz)	120	25	0	0	1	–	0	1	0
Celery (chopped)	¼ cup	5	0.2	1	0.5	0	–	0	1	0
Plain non-fat Greek Yogurt	2 tablespoons	33	5.1	2	0	0	Low	0	1	0
Fresh Dill (chopped)	1 tablespoon	1	0.1	0.2	0.1	0	–	0	1	0
Salt and pepper	To taste	0	0	0	0	0	–	0	–	0
Total		~204	~32.4	~13.2	~2.6	~1				0
Points per Serving									2	0

6. Mediterranean Omelet

This omelet is a protein-packed breakfast option filled with Mediterranean flavors. The combination of spinach, feta cheese, and Kalamata olives creates a savory and satisfying dish that will keep you feeling full and energized. Using a combination of egg whites and one whole egg helps to keep the fat content low while still providing essential nutrients.

Prep Time: *5 minutes* **Cook Time**: *5-7 minutes* **Total Time**: *10-12 minutes* **Servings**: *1*

Ingredients:

- 2 egg whites + 1 whole egg
- ½ cup chopped spinach
- ¼ cup crumbled feta cheese
- 1 tablespoon chopped Kalamata olives
- Salt and pepper to taste

Alternative ingredients for low budget and allergies:

- If feta cheese is unavailable or not preferred, substitute with an equal amount of crumbled goat cheese or ricotta cheese (consider points if using full-fat versions).
- For those with olive allergies, omit the Kalamata olives or substitute with chopped sun-dried tomatoes (not packed in oil).

Directions:

1. In a small bowl, whisk together the egg whites and whole egg. Season with salt and pepper.
2. Heat a non-stick skillet over medium heat.
3. Add the chopped spinach and sauté until wilted, about 2-3 minutes.
4. Pour the egg mixture into the skillet and cook until the edges start to set.
5. Sprinkle the spinach with feta cheese and chopped olives.
6. Carefully fold the omelet in half and cook for another minute or until the eggs are set to your liking.
7. Serve immediately.

Nutritional facts:

Macronutrients:

      Calories: ~250

      Protein: ~20g

      Carbs: ~5g

      Fiber: ~2g

      Fat: ~15g

Micronutrients:

      Vitamin D: negligible

      Calcium: ~100mg

      Iron: ~2mg

      Potassium: ~200mg

Special diet specification and recommendation:

- Suitable for vegetarian diets
- A great option for those looking for a high-protein breakfast.

Chef tips to make it healthier and cook faster:

- Prep the spinach and olives ahead of time to save time in the morning
- Add a pinch of red pepper flakes for a touch of spice
- Serve with a side of sliced tomatoes or a piece of fruit

Recipe Points: 1.5 points

Ingredient	Serving Size	Calories	Protein	Carbs	Fiber	Fat	GI	Points per Serving	Servings Used	Total Points
Egg whites	2	34	8	0	0	0	-	0	1	0
Whole egg	1	70	6	0	0	5	-	0.5	1	0.5
Spinach (cooked)	½ cup	20.5	2.5	3.5	2	0.2	Low	0	1	0
Feta Cheese (crumbled)	¼ cup	100	6	4	0	8	-	1	1	1
Kalamata Olives (chopped)	1 tablespoon	20	0	1	0.5	2	-	0	1	0
Salt and pepper	To taste	0	0	0	0	0	-	0	-	0
Total		~244.5	~22.5	~8.5	~2.5	~15.2				1.5
Points per Serving									1	1.5

7. Lentil and Vegetable Curry

This comforting and aromatic curry is a satisfying and nutritious breakfast option, packed with protein, fiber, and antioxidants. The lentils provide a hearty base, while the mixed vegetables add color, texture, and essential nutrients. The blend of curry powder and turmeric creates a warm and inviting flavor profile, making this a perfect dish for a cozy morning.

Prep Time: *10 minutes* **Cook Time:** *15 minutes* **Total Time:** *25 minutes* **Servings:** *2*

Ingredients:

- 1 cup cooked lentils
- 1 cup mixed vegetables (e.g., carrots, bell peppers, onions), chopped
- 1 tablespoon olive oil
- 1 teaspoon curry powder
- ½ teaspoon turmeric
- Salt and pepper to taste

Alternative ingredients for low budget and allergies:

- If you don't have a specific mix of vegetables, feel free to use whatever you have on hand, such as broccoli, cauliflower, or spinach.
- For those sensitive to spice, reduce the amount of curry powder or omit it altogether.

Directions:

1. Heat the olive oil in a large skillet or saucepan over medium heat.
2. Add the chopped vegetables and sauté until softened, about 5-7 minutes.
3. Add the cooked lentils, curry powder, turmeric, salt, and pepper to the skillet.
4. Stir to combine and cook until heated through, about 5 minutes more.
5. Serve warm with a side of whole-wheat toast or brown rice (consider points for brown rice).

Nutritional facts (per serving):

Macronutrients:

    Calories: ~250

    Protein: ~15g

    Carbs: ~35g

    Fiber: ~10g

    Fat: ~7g

Micronutrients:

    Vitamin D: negligible

    Calcium: ~40mg

    Iron: ~4mg

    Potassium: ~500mg

Special diet specification and recommendation:

- Suitable for vegan and gluten-free diets.
- This dish is a great source of plant-based protein and fiber, making it a filling and satisfying breakfast option.

Chef tips to make it healthier and cook faster:

- Cook a large batch of lentils ahead of time to have on hand for quick meals throughout the week.
- Add a squeeze of lime juice for a touch of brightness.
- Garnish with chopped fresh cilantro or parsley for extra flavor and nutrients.

Recipe Points: 0.6 points

Ingredient	Serving Size	Calories	Protein	Carbs	Fiber	Fat	GI	Points per Serving	Servings Used	Total Points
Lentils (cooked)	1 cup	230	18	40	16	1	Low	0	1	0
Mixed Vegetables (chopped)	1 cup	~50	~2	~10	~3	~0	Low	0	1	0
Olive Oil	1 tablespoon	120	0	0	0	14	-	1.2	1	1.2
Curry powder, Turmeric, Salt, Pepper	-	~0	~0	~0	~0	~0	-	0	-	0
Total		~380	~20	~50	~19	~15				1.2
Points per Serving									2	0.6

8. Smoked Salmon and Avocado Toast

This elegant and flavorful toast is a perfect way to enjoy a special breakfast or brunch. The combination of creamy avocado, smoky salmon, and fresh dill creates a delightful taste and texture experience. It's a quick and easy recipe that is both satisfying and nutritious, providing healthy fats, protein, and essential nutrients.

Prep Time: *5 minutes* **Cook Time**: *2-3 minutes (to toast the bread)* **Total Time**: *7-8 minutes* **Servings**: 1

Ingredients:

- 1 slice whole-wheat toast
- ½ avocado, mashed
- 2 ounces smoked salmon
- Sprinkle of red pepper flakes
- Fresh dill sprig

Alternative ingredients for low budget and allergies:

- If you don't have smoked salmon, you can use canned salmon or another type of smoked fish like mackerel or trout
- If you have an avocado allergy, substitute with hummus or mashed chickpeas

Directions:

1. Toast the whole-wheat bread to your desired level of crispiness
2. While the bread is toasting, mash the avocado in a small bowl
3. Spread the mashed avocado evenly on the toasted bread
4. Top with the smoked salmon
5. Sprinkle with red pepper flakes and garnish with a fresh dill sprig.
6. Serve immediately and enjoy!

Nutritional facts:

Macronutrients:
Calories: ~300
Protein: ~15g
Carbs: ~30g
Fiber: ~7g
Fat: ~15g

Micronutrients:
Vitamin D: negligible
Calcium: ~20mg
Iron: ~1mg
Potassium: ~400mg

Special diet specification and recommendation:

- Suitable for gluten-free diets (if using gluten-free bread)
- A great option for those following a low-carb or keto diet.

Chef tips to make it healthier and faster:

- Use a ripe avocado for easier mashing
- Add a squeeze of lemon juice to the avocado to prevent browning
- If you don't have fresh dill, you can use dried dill or omit it altogether.

Recipe Points: 0 points (all ingredients are from the no-point food list)

Ingredient	Serving Size	Calories	Protein	Carbs	Fiber	Fat	GI	Points per Serving	Servings Used	Total Points
Whole Wheat Toast	1 slice	80	4	15	2	1	Medium	1	1	1
Avocado (mashed)	½ medium	160	2	9	7	15	Low	0	1	0
Smoked Salmon	2 oz	80	12	0	0	4	–	0	1	0
Red Pepper Flakes & Dill	–	~0	~0	~0	~0	~0	–	0	–	0
Total		~320	~18	~24	~9	~20				1
Points per Serving									1	1

9. Berry and Spinach Smoothie:

This vibrant smoothie is a refreshing and nutritious way to start your day. Packed with antioxidants from the berries and spinach, it also offers a good source of protein and healthy fats from the almond milk (or optional Greek yogurt). It's a quick and easy breakfast option that can be customized with your favorite fruits and greens.

Prep Time: 5 minutes **Cook Time**: None **Total Time**: 5 minutes **Servings**: 1

Ingredients:

- 1 cup unsweetened almond milk or water
- 1 cup spinach
- ½ cup mixed berries
- ½ banana

Alternative ingredients for low budget and allergies:

- If you don't have almond milk, water works just as well.
- For those with nut allergies, substitute almond milk with oat milk or another non-dairy milk alternative
- If berries are out of season, you can use frozen berries.
- If you want to add more protein, consider adding a scoop of plain non-fat Greek yogurt.

Directions:

1. Add all ingredients to a blender and blend until smooth.
2. If the smoothie is too thick, add more almond milk or water until you reach the desired consistency
3. Pour into a glass and enjoy immediately!

Nutritional facts:

Macronutrients:
Calories: ~150
Protein: ~5g
Carbs: ~25g
Fiber: ~5g
Fat: ~3g

Micronutrients:

> Vitamin D: negligible (unless using fortified almond milk)
> Calcium: ~50mg (if using fortified almond milk)
> Iron: ~2mg, Potassium: ~400mg

Special diet specification and recommendation:

- Suitable for vegan and gluten-free diets.
- This smoothie is a great option for a quick and healthy breakfast on the go.

Chef tips to make it healthier and faster:

- Prep smoothie packs with the spinach and berries pre-portioned and frozen for even faster mornings
- Add a handful of ice cubes for a chilled smoothie
- If you want to add more healthy fats, consider adding a tablespoon of chia seeds or flaxseed

Recipe Points: 0.75 points

Ingredient	Serving Size	Calories	Protein	Carbs	Fiber	Fat	GI	Points per Serving	Servings Used	Total Points
Unsweetened Almond Milk	1 cup	30	1	1	0	2.5	-	0	1	0
Spinach (raw)	1 cup	7	1	1	1	0	Low	0	1	0
Mixed Berries	½ cup	31	0.5	7	2	0.25	Low	0	1	0
Banana	½ medium	50	0.5	13	1.5	0	Medium	0.5	1	0.5
Total		~118	~3	~22	~4.5	~2.75				0.5
Points per Serving									1	0.5

10. Mediterranean Breakfast Bowl:

This vibrant and flavorful breakfast bowl is a delightful way to start your day with a burst of Mediterranean goodness. The quinoa provides a hearty base of protein and fiber, while the fresh vegetables add crunch and essential nutrients. The feta cheese offers a touch of creamy saltiness, and the olive oil drizzle adds richness and healthy fats.

Prep Time: *10 minutes* **Cook Time:** *15-20 minutes (for cooking quinoa, if not pre-cooked)* **Total Time:** *25-30 minutes* **Servings:** 1

Ingredients:

- ½ cup cooked quinoa
- ½ cup chopped cucumber
- ½ cup cherry tomatoes, halved
- ¼ cup crumbled feta cheese
- 1 tablespoon chopped fresh parsley
- Drizzle of olive oil
- Salt and pepper to taste

Alternative ingredients for low budget and allergies:

- If you don't have quinoa, you can use cooked brown rice or couscous as a base
- If feta cheese is not available or preferred, substitute with an equal amount of crumbled goat cheese or ricotta cheese (consider points if using full-fat versions).

Directions:

1. If you're not using pre-cooked quinoa, cook it according to package directions
2. In a bowl, combine the cooked quinoa, chopped cucumber, halved cherry tomatoes, crumbled feta cheese, and chopped parsley
3. Drizzle with olive oil and season with salt and pepper to taste
4. Toss gently to combine and enjoy!

Nutritional facts:

Macronutrients:

Calories: ~350
Protein: ~12g
Carbs: ~45g
Fiber: ~6g
Fat: ~15g

Micronutrients:

Vitamin D: negligible
Calcium: ~150mg
Iron: ~2mg
Potassium: ~400mg

Special diet specification and recommendation:

- Suitable for vegetarian and gluten-free diets.
- This bowl is a great source of plant-based protein and fiber, keeping you feeling full and energized throughout the morning

Chef tips to make it healthier and faster:

- Cook a large batch of quinoa ahead of time to have on hand for quick meals throughout the week
- Add a squeeze of lemon juice for a touch of brightness
- Top with a fried or poached egg for extra protein (consider points for the egg yolk if applicable)

Recipe Points: 1.5 points

Ingredient	Serving Size	Calories	Protein	Carbs	Fiber	Fat	GI	Points per Serving	Servings Used	Total Points
Quinoa (cooked)	½ cup	111	4	20	2.5	2	Low	0	1	0
Cucumber (chopped)	½ cup	8	0.5	2	0.5	0	-	0	1	0
Cherry Tomatoes (halved)	½ cup	15	1	3	1	0	Low	0	1	0
Feta Cheese (crumbled)	¼ cup	100	6	4	0	8	-	1	1	1
Fresh Parsley (chopped)	1 tablespoon	1	0.1	0.2	0.1	0	-	0	1	0
Olive Oil	Drizzle (let's assume 1 tsp)	40	0	0	0	4.5	-	0.5	1	0.5
Salt and pepper	To taste	0	0	0	0	0	-	0	-	0
Total		~275	~11.6	~29.2	~4.1	~14.5				1.5
Points per Serving									1	1.5

11. Baked Eggs with Spinach and Tomatoes:

This simple yet elegant dish is a delightful way to enjoy a protein-rich breakfast. The eggs are baked in a bed of flavorful spinach and tomatoes, creating a warm and comforting meal that's perfect for a leisurely morning. It's a great option for those who prefer a savory breakfast and want to incorporate more vegetables into their diet.

Prep Time: *5 minutes* **Cook Time**: *15-20 minutes* **Total Time**: *20-25 minutes* **Servings**: *1*

Ingredients:

- 2 eggs
- ½ cup chopped spinach
- ½ cup chopped tomatoes
- Salt and pepper to taste

Alternative ingredients for low budget and allergies:

- If you don't have fresh spinach, you can use frozen spinach, thawed and squeezed dry.
- For a variation, add other vegetables like mushrooms or bell peppers.

Directions:

1. Preheat oven to 350°F (175°C).
2. Lightly grease a ramekin or small baking dish with olive oil.
3. Layer the chopped spinach and tomatoes in the prepared dish.
4. Crack the eggs on top of the vegetables.
5. Season with salt and pepper to taste
6. Bake for 15-20 minutes, or until the egg whites are set and the yolks are cooked to your liking

Nutritional facts:

Macronutrients:

Calories: ~180
Protein: ~12g
Carbs: ~8g
Fiber: ~3g
Fat: ~10g

Micronutrients:

       Vitamin D: ~10% Daily Value

       Calcium: ~50mg

       Iron: ~2mg

       Potassium: ~300mg

Special diet specification and recommendation:

- Suitable for vegetarian and gluten-free diets
- A good source of protein and essential nutrients.

Chef tips to make it healthier and faster:

- Prep the vegetables the night before to save time in the morning
- Add a sprinkle of crumbled feta cheese for extra flavor and calcium
- Serve with a side of whole-wheat toast or a piece of fruit

Recipe Points: 1 point

Ingredient	Serving Size	Calories	Protein	Carbs	Fiber	Fat	GI	Points per Serving	Servings Used	Total Points
Eggs	2 large	140	12	0	0	10	-	1	1	1
Spinach (cooked)	½ cup	20.5	2.5	3.5	2	0.2	Low	0	1	0
Tomatoes (raw)	½ cup	11	0.5	2.5	0.5	0	Low	0	1	0
Salt and pepper	To taste	0	0	0	0	0	-	0	-	0
Total		~171.5	~15	~6	~3	~10.2				1
Points per Serving									1	1

12. Fruit and Yogurt Bowl:

This refreshing and vibrant bowl is a simple yet satisfying breakfast or snack option. The combination of creamy yogurt, sweet fruits, and crunchy almonds provides a delightful balance of flavors and textures. It's a great way to incorporate more fruits into your diet and get a boost of protein and healthy fats.

Prep Time: 5 minutes **Cook Time**: None **Total Time**: 5 minutes **Servings**: 1

Ingredients:

- 1 cup plain non-fat Greek yogurt
- ½ cup mixed berries
- ½ sliced banana
- 1 tablespoon chopped almonds

Alternative ingredients for low budget and allergies:

- If you don't have Greek yogurt, you can use any other type of plain, non-fat yogurt
- For those with nut allergies, substitute the almonds with an equal amount of pumpkin seeds or sunflower seeds.
- Feel free to use any combination of fruits you enjoy, such as sliced peaches, chopped apples, or grapes

Directions:

1. In a bowl, combine the yogurt, mixed berries, sliced banana, and chopped almonds
2. Enjoy immediately

Nutritional facts:

Macronutrients:
Calories: ~250
Protein: ~20g
Carbs: ~30g
Fiber: ~5g
Fat: ~8g

Micronutrients:
Vitamin D: negligible (unless yogurt is fortified)
Calcium: ~200mg
Iron: ~1mg
Potassium: ~500mg

Special diet specification and recommendation:

- Suitable for vegetarian diets
- A great option for a quick and healthy breakfast or snack.

Chef tips to make it healthier and faster:

- Prep the fruit ahead of time and store it in the refrigerator for a grab-and-go breakfast
- Add a sprinkle of chia seeds or flaxseed for extra fiber and omega-3 fatty acids.
- If you want to add more sweetness, drizzle with a small amount of honey or maple syrup (consider points if using).

Recipe Points: 0 points (all ingredients are from the no-point food list)

Ingredient	Serving Size	Calories	Protein	Carbs	Fiber	Fat	GI	Points per Serving	Servings Used	Total Points
Plain non-fat Greek Yogurt	1 cup	100	17	6	0	0	Low	0	1	0
Mixed Berries	½ cup	31	0.5	7	2	0.25	Low	0	1	0
Banana (sliced)	½ medium	50	0.5	13	1.5	0	Medium	0.5	1	0.5
Almonds (chopped)	1 tablespoon	45	1	2	1	4	-	0	1	0
Total		~226	~19	~28	~4.5	~4.25				0.5
Points per Serving									1	0.5

13. Sardine Toast with Tomatoes & Herbs

This simple yet flavorful toast offers a unique and nutritious breakfast or snack option. Sardines are a fantastic source of omega-3 fatty acids, calcium, and vitamin D, while the tomatoes provide antioxidants and vitamins. The fresh basil adds a touch of freshness and herbaceous flavor, making this a delightful and satisfying meal.

Prep Time: *5 minutes* **Cook Time**: *2-3 minutes (to toast the bread)* **Total Time**: *7-8 minutes* **Servings**: *1*

Ingredients:

- 1 slice whole-wheat toast
- 3-4 sardines in olive oil, drained
- ½ sliced tomato
- Fresh basil leaves

Alternative ingredients for low budget and allergies:

- If you don't have sardines, you can use canned salmon or tuna.
- If you have a fish allergy, substitute the sardines with mashed avocado or hummus.
- If fresh basil is not available, you can use dried basil or another fresh herb like parsley or oregano.

Directions:

1. Toast the whole-wheat bread to your desired level of crispiness.
2. While the bread is toasting, arrange the sardines on top.
3. Top with tomato slices and fresh basil leaves
4. Serve immediately and enjoy

Nutritional facts:

Macronutrients:
Calories: ~200
Protein: ~20g
Carbs: ~15g
Fiber: ~3g
Fat: ~8g

Micronutrients:
Vitamin D: ~30% Daily Value (from sardines)
Calcium: ~150mg (from sardines)
Iron: ~2mg
Potassium: ~300mg

Special diet specification and recommendation:

- Suitable for gluten-free diets (if using gluten-free bread)
- A great option for those looking for a high-protein, high-calcium breakfast or snack

Chef tips to make it healthier and faster:

- If you prefer a less fishy flavor, rinse the sardines before using them.
- Add a squeeze of lemon juice for extra brightness
- If you don't have fresh basil, you can use dried basil or another fresh herb like parsley or oregano

Recipe Points: 1 point

Ingredient	Serving Size	Calories	Protein	Carbs	Fiber	Fat	GI	Points per Serving	Servings Used	Total Points
Whole Wheat Toast	1 slice	80	4	15	2	1	Medium	1	1	1
Sardines in olive oil (drained)	3-4	100	16	0	0	6	-	0	1	0
Tomato (sliced)	½ medium	11	0.5	2.5	0.5	0	Low	0	1	0
Fresh Basil	Few leaves	~0	~0	~0	~0	~0	-	0	-	0
Total		~191	~20.5	~17.5	~2.5	~7				1
Points per Serving									1	1

14. Chickpea and Veggie Fritters:

These savory fritters are a delightful and nutritious snack or light meal option. Packed with protein and fiber from the chickpeas, they also incorporate the goodness of zucchini and carrots, adding vitamins, minerals, and a touch of sweetness. The egg white helps bind the mixture, while the fresh parsley adds a burst of freshness and flavor.

Prep Time: *15 minutes* **Cook Time**: *10-12 minutes* **Total Time**: *25-27 minutes* **Servings**: 4

Ingredients:

- 1 cup cooked chickpeas, mashed
- ½ cup grated zucchini
- ¼ cup grated carrot
- 1 egg white
- 1 tablespoon chopped fresh parsley
- Salt and pepper to taste
- Olive oil for cooking

Alternative ingredients for low budget and allergies:

- If you don't have zucchini or carrots, feel free to substitute with other vegetables like grated sweet potato or finely chopped broccoli.
- For those with egg allergies, you can use a flax egg (1 tablespoon ground flaxseed mixed with 3 tablespoons water) as a binder

Directions:

1. In a large bowl, combine the mashed chickpeas, grated zucchini, grated carrot, egg white, and chopped parsley.
2. Season with salt and pepper to taste.
3. Heat a drizzle of olive oil in a large skillet over medium heat
4. Form the mixture into 4 patties.
5. Carefully place the patties in the hot skillet and cook for about 5-6 minutes per side, or until golden brown and cooked through.
6. Serve warm with a dollop of plain yogurt or a side salad.

Macronutrients:
Calories: ~150
Protein: ~8g
Carbs: ~20g
Fiber: ~5g
Fat: ~5g
Micronutrients:
Vitamin D: negligible
Calcium: ~40mg
Iron: ~2mg
Potassium: ~250mg

Special diet specification and recommendation:

- Suitable for vegetarian and gluten-free diets
- A great option for a protein-rich and satisfying snack or light meal

Chef tips to make it healthier and faster:

- Squeeze out excess moisture from the grated zucchini before adding it to the mixture to prevent the fritters from becoming soggy
- If the mixture is too wet, add a bit more breadcrumbs to help it hold its shape
- Serve with a dipping sauce made with plain yogurt, herbs, and spices for extra flavor

Recipe Points: 0.6 points

Ingredient	Serving Size	Calories	Protein	Carbs	Fiber	Fat	GI	Points per Serving	Servings Used	Total Points
Chickpeas (cooked)	1 cup	280	16	48	12	4	Low	0	1	0
Zucchini (grated)	½ cup	10	1	2	1	0	Low	0	1	0
Carrot (grated)	¼ cup	10	0.3	2.5	0.7	0	Low	0	1	0
Egg white	1	17	3.6	0.2	0	0	-	0	1	0
Fresh Parsley (chopped)	1 tablespoon	1	0.1	0.2	0.1	0	-	0	1	0
Salt and pepper	To taste	0	0	0	0	0	-	0	-	0
Olive Oil	For cooking (let's assume 2 tablespoons total)	240	0	0	0	28	-	2.8	1	2.8
Total		~557	~20	~52.7	~13.8	~32				2.8
Points per Serving									4	0.7

15. Apple Cinnamon Cottage Cheese Bowl

This simple and satisfying bowl is a perfect snack or light breakfast option. The cottage cheese provides a good source of protein and calcium, while the apple adds sweetness, fiber, and crunch. The cinnamon adds warmth and spice, making this a comforting and nutritious treat

Prep Time: *5 minutes* **Cook Time:** *None* **Total Time:** *5 minutes* **Servings:** 1

Ingredients:

- 1 cup low-fat cottage cheese
- 1 small apple, chopped
- Sprinkle of cinnamon

Alternative ingredients for low budget and allergies:

- If you don't have low-fat cottage cheese, you can use plain non-fat Greek yogurt
- For those with apple allergies, substitute with another chopped fruit like pears or peaches

Directions:

1. In a bowl, combine the cottage cheese, chopped apple and sprinkle of cinnamon.
2. Enjoy immediately!

Nutritional facts:

Macronutrients:
Calories: ~160
Protein: ~25g
Carbs: ~15g
Fiber: ~3g
Fat: ~2g

Micronutrients:
Vitamin D: negligible
Calcium: ~150mg
Iron: ~1mg
Potassium: ~300mg

Special diet specification and recommendation:

- Suitable for vegetarian and gluten-free diets
- A great option for a high-protein, low-fat snack

Chef tips to make it healthier and faster:

- Prep the chopped apple ahead of time and store it in the refrigerator for a grab-and-go snack.
- Add a handful of chopped walnuts or almonds for extra crunch and healthy fats
- If you want to add more sweetness, drizzle with a small amount of honey or maple syrup (consider points if using).

Recipe Points: 0 points (all ingredients are from the no-point food list)

Ingredient	Serving Size	Calories	Protein	Carbs	Fiber	Fat	GI	Points per Serving	Servings Used	Total Points
Low-fat Cottage Cheese	1 cup	163	28	6	0	2	–	0	1	0
Apple (chopped)	1 small	72	0	19	3	0	Low	0	1	0
Cinnamon	Sprinkle	~0	~0	~0	~0	~0	–	0	–	0
Total		~235	~28	~25	~3	~2				0
Points per Serving									1	0

Mediterranean Lunch & Light Bite Recipes

1. Mediterranean Tuna Salad Lettuce Wraps

These lettuce wraps offer a refreshing and light lunch option that's packed with protein and healthy fats. The tuna provides omega-3 fatty acids, while the vegetables add crunch, vitamins, and minerals. The Greek yogurt adds creaminess without extra fat, and the fresh dill provides a bright, herbaceous note. The lettuce wraps make this a satisfying yet low-carb meal, perfect for a midday pick-me-up.

Prep time: *10 minutes* **Cook time:** *None* **Total time:** *10 minutes* **Servings:** *2*

Ingredients

- 1 can tuna in water, drained
- ¼ cup chopped cucumber
- ¼ cup chopped red onion
- 2 tablespoons plain non-fat Greek yogurt
- 1 tablespoon chopped fresh dill
- Salt and pepper to taste
- Large lettuce leaves (such as romaine or butter lettuce)

Alternative Ingredients for Low Budget and Allergies:

- **Tuna:** Substitute with canned salmon or cooked, shredded chicken breast.
- **Greek Yogurt:** If dairy-free, use a plant-based yogurt alternative.
- **Fresh Dill:** Substitute with dried dill or another fresh herb like parsley or chives.

Directions:

1. In a medium bowl, combine tuna, cucumber, red onion, Greek yogurt, and dill.
2. Season with salt and pepper to taste.

3. Spoon the tuna salad mixture into the lettuce leaves.
4. Roll up the lettuce leaves to create wraps.
5. Enjoy immediately!

Nutritional Facts (per serving):

Macronutrients:
    Calories: ~150
    Protein: ~20g
    Carbs: ~5g
    Fiber: ~2g
    Fat: ~5g

Micronutrients:
    Vitamin D: negligible
    Calcium: ~50mg (from yogurt)
    Iron: ~1mg
    Potassium: ~250mg

Special diet specification and recommendation:

- Suitable for gluten-free and low-carb diets.
- If using dairy-free yogurt, it's also suitable for dairy-free diets.

Chef tips to make it healthier and faster:

- Prep the vegetables ahead of time and store them in airtight containers in the refrigerator for quick assembly.
- Add a squeeze of lemon juice to the tuna salad for extra brightness.
- If you prefer a spicier tuna salad, add a pinch of red pepper flakes or a dash of hot sauce.

Recipe Points: 0 points (all ingredients are from the no-point food list)

Ingredient	Serving Size	Calories	Protein	Carbs	Fiber	Fat	GI	Points per Serving	Servings Used	Total Points
Tuna in water (drained)	½ can (2.5 oz)	60	12.5	0	0	0.5	-	0	1	0
Cucumber (chopped)	¼ cup	4	0.25	1	0.25	0	-	0	1	0
Red Onion (chopped)	¼ cup	16	0.4	4	0.6	0	-	0	1	0
Plain non-fat Greek Yogurt	2 tablespoons	33	5.1	2	0	0	Low	0	1	0
Fresh Dill (chopped)	1 tablespoon	1	0.1	0.2	0.1	0	-	0	1	0
Salt and pepper	To taste	0	0	0	0	0	-	0	-	0
Lettuce leaves		~0	~0	~0	~0	~0	-	0	-	0
Total		~114	~18.35	~7.2	~1.15	~0.5				0
Points per Serving									2	0

2. Lemony Lentil Salad with Herbs

This vibrant and protein-packed salad is a delightful lunch option, brimming with Mediterranean flavors. The lentils offer a hearty base, while the fresh vegetables provide a refreshing crunch and essential nutrients. The lemon juice and herbs add a bright, zesty touch, making this a satisfying and flavorful meal that's perfect for a warm day.

Prep time: 15 minutes **Cook time:** *None (assuming lentils are pre-cooked)* **Total time:** *15 minutes* **Servings:** 4

Ingredients:

- 1 cup cooked lentils
- ½ cup chopped cucumber
- ½ cup chopped tomatoes
- ¼ cup chopped red onion
- ¼ cup chopped fresh parsley
- 1 tablespoon olive oil
- 1 tablespoon lemon juice
- Salt and pepper to taste

Alternative ingredients for low budget and allergies:

- If you don't have fresh parsley, you can use dried parsley or another fresh herb like dill or cilantro
- You can substitute the lentils with another type of cooked legume, such as chickpeas or black beans

Directions:

1. In a large bowl, combine the cooked lentils, chopped cucumber, tomatoes, red onion, and parsley.
2. In a small bowl, whisk together the olive oil, lemon juice, salt, and pepper to make the dressing
3. Pour the dressing over the lentil salad and toss to coat evenly.
4. Serve chilled or at room temperature.

Macronutrients:

    Calories: ~200

    Protein: ~10g

    Carbs: ~25g

    Fiber: ~8g

    Fat: ~7g

Micronutrients:

    Vitamin D: negligible

    Calcium: ~30mg

    Iron: ~3mg

    Potassium: ~400mg

Special diet specification and recommendation:

- Suitable for vegan and gluten-free diets
- A great option for a high-protein, high-fiber, and nutrient-rich lunch

Chef tips to make it healthier and faster:

- Cook a large batch of lentils ahead of time to have on hand for quick meals throughout the week
- Add a pinch of red pepper flakes for a touch of spice
- If you prefer a creamier dressing, add a tablespoon of plain non-fat Greek yogurt to the vinaigrette

Ingredient	Serving Size	Calories	Protein	Carbs	Fiber	Fat	GI	Points per Serving	Servings Used	Total Points
Lentils (cooked)	1 cup	230	18	40	16	1	Low	0	1	0
Cucumber (chopped)	½ cup	8	0.5	2	0.5	0	-	0	1	0
Tomatoes (chopped)	½ cup	11	0.5	2.5	0.5	0	Low	0	1	0
Red Onion (chopped)	¼ cup	16	0.4	4	0.6	0	-	0	1	0
Fresh Parsley (chopped)	¼ cup	2	0.2	0.4	0.2	0	-	0	1	0
Olive Oil	1 tablespoon	120	0	0	0	14	-	1.2	1	1.2
Lemon Juice	1 tablespoon	3	0	1	0	0	-	0	1	0
Salt and pepper	To taste	0	0	0	0	0	-	0	-	0
Total		~390	~19.6	~49.9	~17.8	~15				1.2
Points per Serving									4	0.3

3. Grilled Chicken & Veggie Skewers

These colorful and flavorful skewers are a delightful and healthy lunch or light dinner option. The grilled chicken provides lean protein, while the assortment of vegetables adds vitamins, minerals, and fiber. The simple marinade of olive oil, oregano, salt, and pepper enhances the natural flavors of the ingredients, making this a satisfying and nutritious meal that's perfect for a warm day.

Prep time: *15 minutes* **Cook time:** *10-12 minutes* **Total time:** *25-27 minutes* **Servings:** 4

Ingredients

- 1 boneless, skinless chicken breast, cut into cubes
- 1 bell pepper, cut into chunks
- 1 zucchini, cut into chunks
- 1 red onion, cut into chunks
- 1 tablespoon olive oil
- Dried oregano, salt, and pepper to taste

Alternative ingredients for low budget and allergies:

- **Chicken:** Substitute with firm tofu cubes or tempeh cubes, marinated in the same way
- **Vegetables:** Feel free to use any combination of your favorite vegetables, such as mushrooms, cherry tomatoes, or eggplant.

Directions:

1. Thread the chicken cubes, bell pepper chunks, zucchini chunks, and red onion chunks onto skewers, alternating between the ingredients
2. In a small bowl, whisk together the olive oil, dried oregano, salt, and pepper to make the marinade
3. Brush the skewers generously with the marinade
4. Preheat the grill to medium-high heat
5. Place the skewers on the grill and cook for 10-12 minutes, or until the chicken is cooked through and the vegetables are tender-crisp, turning occasionally

Nutritional facts (per serving):

Macronutrients:

      Calories: ~200

      Protein: ~25g

      Carbs: ~10g

      Fiber: ~3g

      Fat: ~8g

Micronutrients:

      Vitamin D: negligible

      Calcium: ~30mg

      Iron: ~2mg

      Potassium: ~400mg

Special diet specification and recommendation:

- Suitable for gluten-free diets
- Can be easily adapted for vegetarian or vegan diets by substituting the chicken with tofu or tempeh

Chef tips to make it healthier and faster:

- Soak the skewers in water for 30 minutes before assembling to prevent them from burning on the grill
- Marinate the chicken and vegetables for at least 30 minutes, or up to overnight, for maximum flavor
- Serve with a side of brown rice or quinoa (consider points if applicable) and a dollop of tzatziki for a complete meal

Recipe Points: 0.3 points per serving

Ingredient	Serving Size	Calories	Protein	Carbs	Fiber	Fat	GI	Points per Serving	Servings Used	Total Points
Chicken Breast (boneless, skinless)	3 oz	140	26	0	0	3	–	0	1	0
Bell Pepper	1 medium	30	1	7	2	0	Low	0	1	0
Zucchini	1 medium	33	2	6	2	0.4	Low	0	1	0
Red Onion	1 medium	64	1.5	15	2	0	–	0	1	0
Olive Oil	1 tablespoon	120	0	0	0	14	–	1.2	1	1.2
Dried Oregano, Salt, Pepper	–	~0	~0	~0	~0	~0	–	0	–	0
Total		~387	~30.5	~28	~6	~17.4				1.2
Points per Serving									4	0.3

4. Hummus & Veggie Pita Pockets

These pita pockets are a quick, easy, and satisfying lunch option that's packed with flavor and nutrients. The whole-wheat pitas provide fiber and complex carbohydrates, while the hummus offers a creamy and protein-rich filling. The fresh vegetables add crunch, vitamins, and minerals, making this a well-rounded and delicious meal.

Prep Time: 10 minutes **Cook Time**: None **Total Time**: 10 minutes **Servings**: 2

Ingredients:

- 2 whole-wheat pitas
- ½ cup hummus (ensure it's made with zero-point ingredients like chickpeas, tahini, olive oil, and lemon juice)
- 1 cup mixed greens
- ½ cup sliced cucumber
- ½ cup sliced bell peppers

Alternative ingredients for low budget and allergies:

- **Pitas:** If whole-wheat pitas are unavailable or you have a gluten intolerance, you can use large lettuce leaves or collard greens as wraps instead
- **Hummus:** If you don't have hummus or prefer a different flavor, you can substitute it with mashed avocado or another bean dip made with zero-point ingredients

Directions:

1. If desired, warm the pitas in a toaster or skillet for a few seconds until slightly softened
2. Cut a slit lengthwise in each pita to create a pocket
3. Spread ¼ cup of hummus inside each pita
4. Fill the pitas with mixed greens, sliced cucumber, and bell peppers
5. Enjoy immediately!

Macronutrients:

Calories: ~300

Protein: ~12g

Carbs: ~45g

Fiber: ~10g

Fat: ~10g

Micronutrients:

Vitamin D: negligible

Calcium: ~50mg

Iron: ~3mg

Potassium: ~500mg

Special diet specification and recommendation:

- Can be easily adapted for vegan and gluten-free diets (by using appropriate pita substitutes).
- A great option for a quick and easy lunch on the go

Chef tips to make it healthier and faster:

- Prep the vegetables ahead of time and store them in airtight containers in the refrigerator for quick assembly.
- Add a drizzle of olive oil and a squeeze of lemon juice to the hummus for extra flavor
- If you want to add more protein, consider adding grilled chicken or chickpeas to the pita pockets

Ingredient	Serving Size	Calories	Protein	Carbs	Fiber	Fat	GI	Points per Serving	Servings Used	Total Points
Whole Wheat Pitas	2	160	8	30	4	2	Medium	1.5	1	1.5
Hummus (zero-point)	½ cup	200	8	20	6	10	Low	0	1	0
Mixed Greens	1 cup	7	1	1	1	0	Low	0	1	0
Cucumber (sliced)	½ cup	8	0.5	2	0.5	0	-	0	1	0
Bell Peppers (sliced)	½ cup	15	0.5	3.5	1	0	Low	0	1	0
Total		~390	~18	~56.5	~12.5	~12				1.5
Points per Serving									2	0.75

5. Caprese Salad

This classic Italian salad is a simple yet elegant dish that celebrates the fresh flavors of summer. The juicy tomatoes, creamy mozzarella, and fragrant basil create a perfect harmony of tastes and textures. Drizzled with balsamic vinegar and olive oil, this salad is a light and refreshing lunch or side dish that's perfect for any occasion.

Prep Time: 10 minutes **Cook Time**: None **Total Time**: 10 minutes **Servings**: 2

Ingredients:

- 2 large tomatoes, sliced
- ½ cup fresh mozzarella, sliced (part-skim or low-fat)
- Fresh basil leaves
- Drizzle of balsamic vinegar
- Drizzle of olive oil
- Salt and pepper to taste

Alternative ingredients for low budget and allergies:

- **Mozzarella:** If you're watching your points or have dietary restrictions, you can omit the mozzarella or substitute it with a small amount of crumbled feta cheese.
- **Fresh Basil:** If fresh basil is unavailable, you can use dried basil or substitute with another fresh herb like oregano or parsley

Directions:

1. Arrange the sliced tomatoes and mozzarella on a plate, alternating between the two.
2. Tuck fresh basil leaves between the tomato and mozzarella slices
3. Drizzle with balsamic vinegar and olive oil
4. Season with salt and pepper to taste
5. Serve immediately

Nutritional facts (per serving):

Macronutrients:

    Calories: ~200

    Protein: ~10g

    Carbs: ~15g

    Fiber: ~3g

    Fat: ~12g

Micronutrients:

    Vitamin D: negligible

    Calcium: ~200mg

    Iron: ~1mg

    Potassium: ~300mg

Special diet specification and recommendation:

- Suitable for vegetarian and gluten-free diets.
- If omitting the mozzarella, this salad is also suitable for vegan and dairy-free diets

Chef tips to make it healthier and faster:

- Use ripe, juicy tomatoes for the best flavor
- Choose part-skim or low-fat mozzarella to reduce the fat and calorie content
- Add a drizzle of pesto for extra flavor (consider points if using).

Recipe Points: 0.5 points per serving

Ingredient	Serving Size	Calories	Protein	Carbs	Fiber	Fat	GI	Points per Serving	Servings Used	Total Points
Tomatoes (sliced)	1 large	22	1	5	1	0	Low	0	2	0
Fresh Mozzarella (part-skim, sliced)	½ cup	125	15	3	0	4	-	0.5	1	0.5
Fresh Basil	Few leaves	~0	~0	~0	~0	~0	-	0	-	0
Balsamic Vinegar	Drizzle (let's assume 1 tsp)	3	0	1	0	0	-	0	1	0
Olive Oil	Drizzle (let's assume 1 tsp)	40	0	0	0	4.5	-	0.5	1	0.5
Salt and pepper	To taste	0	0	0	0	0	-	0	-	0
Total		~190	~16	~9	~1	~8.5				1
Points per Serving									2	0.5

6. Black Bean & Corn Salad

This vibrant and flavorful salad is a fiesta of textures and tastes, combining the heartiness of black beans with the sweetness of corn. It's a refreshing and nutritious lunch option, packed with protein, fiber, and essential vitamins and minerals. The lime juice and cilantro add a zesty touch, while the olive oil provides healthy fats.

Prep time: 15 minutes **Cook time**: *None (if using canned/frozen corn)* **Total time**: *15 minutes* **Servings**: 4

Ingredients:

- 1 can black beans, rinsed and drained
- 1 cup frozen or fresh corn kernels
- ½ cup chopped red onion
- ½ cup chopped bell pepper
- 1 tablespoon olive oil
- 1 tablespoon lime juice
- Chopped cilantro to taste
- Salt and pepper to taste

Alternative ingredients for low budget and allergies:

- If you prefer a different type of bean, you can substitute black beans with chickpeas or kidney beans.
- If fresh cilantro is not available or preferred, you can use dried cilantro or substitute with another fresh herb like parsley.

Directions:

1. If using frozen corn, thaw it according to package instructions. If using fresh corn, remove the kernels from the cob
2. In a large bowl, combine the black beans, corn kernels, red onion, bell pepper, and cilantro
3. In a small bowl, whisk together the olive oil, lime juice, salt, and pepper to make the dressing
4. Pour the dressing over the salad and toss to coat evenly
5. Serve chilled or at room temperature

Nutritional facts (per serving):

Macronutrients:
Calories: ~230
Protein: ~10g
Carbs: ~35g
Fiber: ~8g
Fat: ~7g

Micronutrients:
Vitamin D: negligible
Calcium: ~40mg
Iron: ~3mg
Potassium: ~450mg

Special diet specification and recommendation:

- Suitable for vegan and gluten-free diets.
- This salad is a great source of plant-based protein and fiber, making it a filling and satisfying lunch option.

Chef tips to make it healthier and faster:

- Use pre-cooked or canned black beans to save time
- If you prefer a spicier salad, add a pinch of cayenne pepper or chopped jalapeño to the dressing.
- Serve with a side of whole-wheat tortillas or pita bread for a more complete meal (consider points if applicable)

Ingredient	Serving Size	Calories	Protein	Carbs	Fiber	Fat	GI	Points per Serving	Servings Used	Total Points
Black Beans (cooked)	1 can (15 oz)	340	24	60	18	3	Low	0	1	0
Corn Kernels	1 cup	125	5	27	4	1.5	Medium	1	1	1
Red Onion (chopped)	½ cup	32	0.8	8	1.2	0	-	0	1	0
Bell Pepper (chopped)	½ cup	15	0.5	3.5	1	0	Low	0	1	0
Olive Oil	1 tablespoon	120	0	0	0	14	-	1.2	1	1.2
Lime Juice	1 tablespoon	3	0	1	0	0	-	0	1	0
Cilantro, Salt and Pepper	To taste	~0	~0	~0	~0	~0	-	0	-	0
Total		~635	~30.3	~99.5	~24.2	~18.5				2.2
Points per Serving									4	0.55

7. Mediterranean Quinoa Bowl

This vibrant and wholesome bowl is a celebration of Mediterranean flavors and textures. The quinoa provides a complete protein and a hearty base, while the fresh vegetables add crunch and essential nutrients. The Kalamata olives and feta cheese offer a briny and salty touch, while the olive oil drizzle adds richness and healthy fats. It's a satisfying and nutritious lunch or light dinner option that's perfect for any occasion.

Prep Time: *10 minutes* **Cook Time:** *15-20 minutes (for cooking quinoa, if not pre-cooked)* **Total Time:** *25-30 minutes* **Servings:** *2*

Ingredients:

- 1 cup cooked quinoa
- ½ cup chopped cucumber
- ½ cup cherry tomatoes, halved
- ¼ cup Kalamata olives, pitted and halved
- 2 tablespoons crumbled feta cheese
- 1 tablespoon chopped fresh parsley
- Drizzle of olive oil
- Salt and pepper to taste

Alternative ingredients for low budget and allergies:

- If you don't have quinoa, you can use cooked brown rice or couscous as a base.
- If feta cheese is not available or preferred, substitute with an equal amount of crumbled goat cheese or omit it altogether.
- If you don't have Kalamata olives, you can use any other type of olive or omit them altogether

Directions:

1. If you're not using pre-cooked quinoa, cook it according to package directions
2. In a bowl, combine the cooked quinoa, chopped cucumber, halved cherry tomatoes, Kalamata olives, crumbled feta cheese, and chopped parsley.
3. Drizzle with olive oil and season with salt and pepper to taste
4. Toss gently to combine.
5. Serve chilled or at room temperature.

Nutritional facts (per serving):

Macronutrients:

Calories: ~250

Protein: ~8g

Carbs: ~30g

Fiber: ~5g

Fat: ~12g

Micronutrients:

Vitamin D: negligible

Calcium: ~75mg

Iron: ~2mg

Potassium: ~300mg

Special diet specification and recommendation:

- Suitable for vegetarian and gluten-free diets.
- A great option for a light and refreshing lunch or dinner, packed with nutrients and healthy fats

Chef tips to make it healthier and faster:

- Cook a large batch of quinoa ahead of time to have on hand for quick meals throughout the week.
- Add a squeeze of lemon juice for a touch of brightness
- Top with grilled chicken or fish for extra protein (consider points if applicable)

Recipe Points: 0.75 points per serving

Ingredient	Serving Size	Calories	Protein	Carbs	Fiber	Fat	GI	Points per Serving	Servings Used	Total Points
Quinoa (cooked)	1 cup	222	8	40	5	4	Low	0	1	0
Cucumber (chopped)	½ cup	8	0.5	2	0.5	0	-	0	1	0
Cherry Tomatoes (halved)	½ cup	15	1	3	1	0	Low	0	1	0
Kalamata Olives (pitted & halved)	¼ cup	50	0	1	1	5	-	0	1	0
Feta Cheese (crumbled)	2 tablespoons	67	4	3	0	5.3	-	0.7	1	0.7
Fresh Parsley (chopped)	1 tablespoon	1	0.1	0.2	0.1	0	-	0	1	0
Olive Oil	Drizzle (let's assume 1.5 tsp total)	60	0	0	0	6.75	-	0.75	1	0.75
Salt and pepper	To taste	0	0	0	0	0	-	0	-	0
Total		~418	~13.6	~46.2	~6.6	~21.05				1.45
Points per Serving									2	0.725

8. Spinach & Strawberry Salad with Balsamic Vinaigrette:

This vibrant and refreshing salad is a delightful combination of sweet and savory flavors. The spinach provides a wealth of vitamins and minerals, while the strawberries add natural sweetness and antioxidants. The almonds offer a satisfying crunch and a dose of healthy fats. The simple balsamic vinaigrette ties everything together with a tangy and flavorful touch.

Prep Time: *10 minutes* **Cook Time**: *None* **Total Time**: *10 minutes* **Servings**: *2*

Ingredients

- 2 cups fresh spinach
- 1 cup sliced strawberries
- ¼ cup slivered almonds
- 1 tablespoon balsamic vinegar
- 1 teaspoon olive oil
- Salt and pepper to taste

Alternative Ingredients for Low Budget and Allergies:

- **Spinach:** Substitute with any other leafy green, such as romaine lettuce or arugula.
- **Strawberries:** Use any other seasonal fruit like blueberries, raspberries, or chopped peaches.
- **Almonds:** Substitute with walnuts, pecans, or sunflower seeds for a different crunch.

Directions:

1. In a large bowl, combine spinach and strawberries.
2. In a small bowl, whisk together balsamic vinegar, olive oil, salt, and pepper to create the vinaigrette.
3. Pour the vinaigrette over the salad and toss to coat evenly
4. Top with slivered almonds.
5. Serve immediately

Macronutrients:

Calories: ~200

Protein: ~5g

Carbs: ~20g

Fiber: ~5g

Fat: ~13g

Micronutrients:

Vitamin D: negligible

Calcium: ~50mg

Iron: ~2mg

Potassium: ~350mg

Special diet specification and recommendation:

- Suitable for vegan and gluten-free diets
- A great option for a light and refreshing lunch or side dish

Chef tips to make it healthier and faster:

- Wash and dry the spinach ahead of time to save on prep.
- Toast the almonds lightly for added flavor and crunch.
- If you prefer a creamier dressing, you can whisk in a tablespoon of plain non-fat Greek yogurt to the vinaigrette.

Recipe Points: 0.5 points per serving

Ingredient	Serving Size	Calories	Protein	Carbs	Fiber	Fat	GI	Points per Serving	Servings Used	Total Points
Spinach (raw)	2 cups	14	2	2	2	0	Low	0	1	0
Strawberries (sliced)	1 cup	46	1	11	3	0.4	Low	0	1	0
Almonds (slivered)	¼ cup	207	7	8	4	18	-	2	1	2
Balsamic Vinegar	1 tablespoon	14	0	3	0	0	-	0	1	0
Olive Oil	1 teaspoon	40	0	0	0	4.5	-	0.5	1	0.5
Salt and pepper	To taste	0	0	0	0	0	-	0	-	0
Total		~317	~10	~24	~9	~22.9				2.5
Points per Serving									2	1.25

9. Salmon Salad Sandwich on Whole Wheat

This satisfying sandwich is a quick and easy lunch option that's packed with protein and healthy fats. The canned salmon provides omega-3 fatty acids and vitamin D, while the Greek yogurt adds creaminess without extra fat. The fresh dill and celery add a refreshing crunch and flavor. It's a perfect way to enjoy a nutritious and delicious meal on the go.

Prep Time: *5 minutes* **Cook Time:** *None* **Total Time:** *5 minutes* **Servings:** 1

Ingredients:

- 2 slices whole-wheat bread
- 3 oz canned salmon, drained and flaked
- 2 tablespoons plain non-fat Greek yogurt
- 1 tablespoon chopped celery
- 1 tablespoon chopped fresh dill
- Salt and pepper to taste
- Lettuce leaves

Alternative Ingredients for Low Budget and Allergies:

- **Salmon:** Substitute with canned tuna or cooked, shredded chicken breast
- **Greek Yogurt:** If dairy-free, use a plant-based yogurt alternative.
- **Fresh Dill:** Substitute with dried dill or another fresh herb like parsley or chives

Directions:

1. In a medium bowl, combine the flaked salmon, Greek yogurt, celery, and dill.
2. Season with salt and pepper to taste
3. Spread the salmon salad mixture evenly on one slice of whole-wheat bread
4. Top with lettuce leaves and the other slice of bread.
5. Enjoy!

Nutritional Facts:

Macronutrients:
Calories: ~300

Protein: ~25g

Carbs: ~30g

Fiber: ~5g

Fat: ~10g

Micronutrients:
Vitamin D: ~40% Daily Value (from salmon)

Calcium: ~100mg

Iron: ~2mg

Potassium: ~400mg

Special diet specification and recommendation:

- Easily adaptable for gluten-free diets (use gluten-free bread)
- A great option for a high-protein, satisfying lunch

Chef tips to make it healthier and faster:

- Toast the bread for a crispier sandwich
- Add a squeeze of lemon juice to the salmon salad for a touch of brightness.
- If you prefer a spicier salmon salad, add a pinch of red pepper flakes or a dash of hot sauce.

Recipe Points: 1.5 points

Ingredient	Serving Size	Calories	Protein	Carbs	Fiber	Fat	GI	Points per Serving	Servings Used	Total Points
Whole Wheat Bread	2 slices	160	8	30	4	2	Medium	1.5	1	1.5
Canned Salmon (drained)	3 oz	120	20	0	0	5	-	0	1	0
Plain non-fat Greek Yogurt	2 tablespoons	33	5.1	2	0	0	Low	0	1	0
Celery (chopped)	1 tablespoon	2	0.1	0.3	0.2	0	-	0	1	0
Fresh Dill (chopped)	1 tablespoon	1	0.1	0.2	0.1	0	-	0	1	0
Salt and Pepper	To taste	0	0	0	0	0	-	0	-	0
Lettuce Leaves		~0	~0	~0	~0	~0	-	0	-	0
Total		~316	~33.3	~32.5	~4.3	~7				1.5
Points per Serving									1	1.5

10. Mediterranean White Bean Dip with Veggies

This creamy and flavorful dip is a perfect healthy snack or light lunch option. The cannellini beans provide a good source of protein and fiber, while the olive oil adds healthy fats. The lemon juice, garlic, and oregano create a bright and zesty flavor profile that complements the fresh vegetables perfectly.

Prep time: 10 minutes **Cook time**: None **Total time**: 10 minutes **Servings**: 4

Ingredients:

- 1 can cannellini beans, rinsed and drained
- 2 tablespoons olive oil
- 1 tablespoon lemon juice
- 2 cloves garlic, minced
- ½ teaspoon dried oregano
- Salt and pepper to taste
- Assorted raw vegetables for dipping (carrots, bell peppers, cucumber slices)

Alternative ingredients for low budget and allergies:

- **Cannellini Beans:** Substitute with any other white bean variety, such as Great Northern beans or navy beans
- **Olive Oil:** If you prefer a milder flavor, you can use avocado oil instead

Directions:

1. In a food processor or blender, combine the cannellini beans, olive oil, lemon juice, garlic, and oregano
2. Process or blend until smooth and creamy, adding a little water if needed to reach desired consistency.
3. Season with salt and pepper to taste
4. Serve with assorted raw vegetables for dipping

Macronutrients:

Calories: ~150

Protein: ~6g

Carbs: ~15g

Fiber: ~5g

Fat: ~8g

Micronutrients:

Vitamin D: negligible

Calcium: ~50mg

Iron: ~2mg

Potassium: ~300mg

Special diet specification and recommendation:

- Suitable for vegan and gluten-free diets
- A great option for a high-protein, high-fiber snack

Chef tips to make it healthier and faster:

- If you don't have a food processor or blender, you can mash the beans with a fork or potato masher until mostly smooth.
- Add a pinch of red pepper flakes for a touch of spice.
- Garnish with chopped fresh parsley or a drizzle of extra virgin olive oil for added flavor and visual appeal

Ingredient	Serving Size	Calories	Protein	Carbs	Fiber	Fat	GI	Points per Serving	Servings Used	Total Points
Cannellini Beans (cooked)	1 can (15 oz)	350	20	62	15	3.5	Low	0	1	0
Olive Oil	2 tablespoons	240	0	0	0	28	-	2.8	1	2.8
Lemon Juice	1 tablespoon	3	0	1	0	0	-	0	1	0
Garlic (minced)	2 cloves	9	0.5	2	0.2	0	-	0	1	0
Dried Oregano	½ teaspoon	2	0.1	0.4	0.2	0.1	-	0	1	0
Salt and Pepper	To taste	0	0	0	0	0	-	0	-	0
Raw Vegetables (for dipping)	-	~0	~0	~0	~0	~0	-	0	-	0
Total		~604	~20.6	~65.4	~15.4	~31.6				2.8
Points per Serving									4	0.7

11. Shrimp & Veggie Stir-fry

This quick and flavorful stir-fry is a light and healthy meal, packed with protein from the shrimp and a variety of nutrients from the colorful vegetables. The simple seasoning of garlic and soy sauce (or tamari) enhances the natural flavors of the ingredients, making this a satisfying and delicious dish that's ready in minutes.

Prep Time: 10 minutes **Cook Time**: 10-12 minutes **Total Time**: 20-22 minutes **Servings**: 2

Ingredients:

- ½ lb shrimp, peeled and deveined
- 1 cup mixed vegetables (broccoli florets, bell pepper strips, snap peas)
- 1 tablespoon olive oil
- 1 clove garlic, minced
- Soy sauce or tamari to taste (use sparingly, consider points)

Alternative ingredients for low budget and allergies:

- **Shrimp:** Substitute with firm tofu cubes or tempeh cubes, marinated in a similar way
- **Mixed Vegetables:** Use any combination of your favorite stir-fry vegetables, such as carrots, mushrooms, or baby corn

Directions:

1. Heat the olive oil in a large skillet or wok over medium-high heat
2. Add the minced garlic and cook until fragrant, about 30 seconds
3. Add the shrimp and vegetables to the skillet and stir-fry until the shrimp is cooked through and the vegetables are crisp-tender, about 5-7 minutes
4. Season with soy sauce or tamari to taste. (Remember that soy sauce and tamari contain sodium, so use sparingly)
5. Serve immediately over cooked brown rice or quinoa (consider points if applicable)

Nutritional facts (per serving):

Macronutrients:

    Calories: ~250

    Protein: ~25g

    Carbs: ~15g

    Fiber: ~4g

    Fat: ~10g

Micronutrients:

    Vitamin D: negligible

    Calcium: ~50mg

    Iron: ~3mg

    Potassium: ~400mg

Special diet specification and recommendation:

- Suitable for gluten-free diets.
- Can be easily adapted for vegetarian or vegan diets by substituting the shrimp with tofu or tempeh

Chef tips to make it healthier and faster:

- Prep the vegetables ahead of time and store them in airtight containers in the refrigerator for quick cooking
- If you don't have fresh garlic, you can use garlic powder
- To add more depth of flavor, consider adding a pinch of ginger or red pepper flakes to the stir-fry

Recipe Points: 0.6 points per serving

Ingredient	Serving Size	Calories	Protein	Carbs	Fiber	Fat	GI	Points per Serving	Servings Used	Total Points
Shrimp (peeled and deveined)	½ lb	250	50	0	0	5	-	0	1	0
Mixed Vegetables	1 cup	~50	~2	~10	~3	~0	Low	0	1	0
Olive Oil	1 tablespoon	120	0	0	0	14	-	1.2	1	1.2
Garlic (minced)	1 clove	4.5	0.2	1	0.1	0	-	0	1	0
Soy Sauce/Tamari	To taste (let's assume 1 tsp)	3	0.5	0.6	0	0	-	0	1	0
Total		~427.5	~52.7	~11.6	~3.1	~19				1.2
Points per Serving									2	0.6

12. Egg Salad Lettuce Wraps

These lettuce wraps offer a light and refreshing twist on the classic egg salad sandwich. The hard-boiled eggs provide a good source of protein, while the Greek yogurt adds creaminess without extra fat. The fresh chives add a delicate onion flavor, making this a satisfying and nutritious lunch or snack option.

Prep Time: *10 minutes (plus time to hard-boil eggs)* **Cook Time:** *10-12 minutes (to hard-boil eggs)* **Total Time:** *20-22 minutes* **Servings:** *2*

Ingredients

- 2 hard-boiled eggs, chopped
- 2 tablespoons plain non-fat Greek yogurt
- 1 tablespoon chopped celery
- 1 tablespoon chopped fresh chives
- Salt and pepper to taste
- Large lettuce leaves (such as romaine or butter lettuce)

Alternative Ingredients for Low Budget and Allergies:

- **Eggs:** If you have an egg allergy, substitute with mashed avocado or hummus.
- **Greek Yogurt:** If dairy-free, use a plant-based yogurt alternative.
- **Fresh Chives:** Substitute with dried chives or another fresh herb like parsley or dill

Directions

1. In a medium bowl, combine the chopped hard-boiled eggs, Greek yogurt, celery, and chives
2. Season with salt and pepper to taste
3. Spoon the egg salad mixture into the lettuce leaves
4. Roll up the lettuce leaves to create wraps.
5. Enjoy immediately!

Nutritional Facts (per serving):

Macronutrients:
> Calories: ~170
> Protein: ~12g
> Carbs: ~5g
> Fiber: ~1g
> Fat: ~10g

Micronutrients:
> Vitamin D: ~10% Daily Value (from eggs)
> Calcium: ~60mg
> Iron: ~1mg
> Potassium: ~150mg

Special diet specification and recommendation

- Suitable for gluten-free and low-carb diets
- If using dairy-free yogurt, also suitable for dairy-free diets

Chef Tips to Make it Healthier and Faster:

- Hard-boil the eggs in advance to save time
- Add a pinch of paprika or cayenne pepper for a touch of spice
- Serve with a side salad or some fresh fruit for a more complete meal

Recipe Points: 0 points (all ingredients are from the no-point food list)

Ingredient	Serving Size	Calories	Protein	Carbs	Fiber	Fat	GI	Points per Serving	Servings Used	Total Points
Hard-boiled Eggs (pg 197) (chopped)	2	142	12	1	0	10	-	0	1	0
Plain non-fat Greek Yogurt	2 tablespoons	33	5.1	2	0	0	Low	0	1	0
Celery (chopped)	1 tablespoon	2	0.1	0.3	0.2	0	-	0	1	0
Fresh Chives (chopped)	1 tablespoon	1	0.1	0.2	0.1	0	-	0	1	0
Salt and Pepper	To taste	0	0	0	0	0	-	0	-	0
Lettuce Leaves		~0	~0	~0	~0	~0	-	0	-	0
Total		~178	~17.3	~3.5	~0.3	~10				0
Points per Serving									2	0

13. Grilled Chicken Caesar Salad

This classic salad gets a healthy makeover with grilled chicken breast and a lightened-up Caesar dressing made with Greek yogurt. It's a satisfying and protein-packed lunch option that's full of flavor and crunch. The romaine lettuce provides essential vitamins and minerals, while the grilled chicken offers lean protein. The homemade dressing adds a creamy and tangy touch without the excess calories and fat of traditional Caesar dressing.

Prep Time: *15 minutes* **Cook Time:** *10-12 minutes (for grilling chicken)* **Total Time:** *25-27 minutes* **Servings:** *2*

Ingredients:

- 3 oz grilled chicken breast, sliced
- 2 cups romaine lettuce, chopped
- 2 tablespoons plain non-fat Greek yogurt
- 1 teaspoon lemon juice
- ½ teaspoon Dijon mustard
- Pinch of garlic powder
- Salt and pepper to taste

Alternative Ingredients for Low Budget and Allergies:

- **Chicken:** Substitute with grilled or baked fish, such as salmon or cod.
- **Greek Yogurt:** If dairy-free, use a plant-based yogurt alternative.
- **Dijon Mustard:** If you don't have Dijon mustard, you can use a small amount of yellow mustard or omit it altogether

Directions:

1. Season the chicken breast with salt and pepper and grill over medium heat for 5-7 minutes per side, or until cooked through. Let it rest for a few minutes, then slice it.
2. In a small bowl, whisk together the Greek yogurt, lemon juice, Dijon mustard, garlic powder, salt, and pepper to make the dressing
3. In a large bowl, combine the chopped romaine lettuce and sliced grilled chicken.
4. Pour the dressing over the salad and toss to coat evenly.
5. Serve immediately.

Macronutrients:

       Calories: ~200

       Protein: ~28g

       Carbs: ~5g

       Fiber: ~2g

       Fat: ~5g

Micronutrients:

       Vitamin D: negligible

       Calcium: ~100mg

       Iron: ~2mg

       Potassium: ~400mg

Special diet specification and recommendation:

- Suitable for gluten-free diets
- A great option for a high-protein, low-carb lunch

Chef tips to make it healthier and faster:

- Grill the chicken breast ahead of time and store it in the refrigerator for quick assembly
- Add a sprinkle of parmesan cheese for extra flavor (consider points if using).
- If you prefer a creamier dressing, you can add an additional tablespoon of Greek yogurt.

Recipe Points: 0 points (all ingredients are from the no-point food list)

Ingredient	Serving Size	Calories	Protein	Carbs	Fiber	Fat	GI	Points per Serving	Servings Used	Total Points
Grilled Chicken Breast (sliced)	3 oz	140	26	0	0	3	-	0	1	0
Romaine Lettuce (chopped)	2 cups	16	1	3	2	0	Low	0	1	0
Plain non-fat Greek Yogurt	2 tablespoons	33	5.1	2	0	0	Low	0	1	0
Lemon Juice	1 teaspoon	1	0	0.3	0	0	-	0	1	0
Dijon Mustard	½ teaspoon	3	0.1	0.6	0	0	-	0	1	0
Garlic Powder, Salt, and Pepper	Pinch	~0	~0	~0	~0	~0	-	0	-	0
Total		~193	~32.2	~3.9	~2	~3				0
Points per Serving									2	0

14. Lentil Soup

This hearty and comforting soup is a perfect meal for a chilly evening. Lentils, packed with protein and fiber, create a satisfying base, while the vegetables add depth and texture. The simple seasoning of olive oil, thyme, and salt and pepper allows the natural flavors of the ingredients to shine through. It's a nourishing and flavorful dish that's easy to make and perfect for the whole family

Prep Time: 10 minutes **Cook Time**: 20-25 minutes ***Total Time***: 30-35 minutes **Servings**: 4

Ingredients:

- 1 cup cooked lentils
- 1 cup chopped vegetables (carrots, celery, onion)
- 4 cups vegetable broth
- 1 tablespoon olive oil
- ½ teaspoon dried thyme
- Salt and pepper to taste

Alternative ingredients for low budget and allergies:

- Feel free to use any combination of vegetables you have on hand, such as potatoes, bell peppers, or spinach
- If you don't have dried thyme, you can substitute with another dried herb like rosemary or oregano.

Directions:

1. Heat the olive oil in a large pot over medium heat
2. Add the chopped vegetables and sauté until softened, about 5-7 minutes
3. Add the cooked lentils, vegetable broth, dried thyme, salt, and pepper to the pot.
4. Bring to a boil, then reduce heat to low and simmer for 20-25 minutes, or until the vegetables are tender.
5. Serve warm with a side of whole-wheat bread or a dollop of plain yogurt (consider points if applicable).

Macronutrients:

Calories: ~200

Protein: ~12g

Carbs: ~30g

Fiber: ~10g

Fat: ~5g

Micronutrients:

Vitamin D: negligible

Calcium: ~40mg

Iron: ~3mg

Potassium: ~500mg

Special diet specification and recommendation:

- Suitable for vegan and gluten-free diets.
- A great option for a hearty and comforting meal that's packed with nutrients

Chef tips to make it healthier and faster:

- Cook a large batch of lentils ahead of time to have on hand for quick meals throughout the week
- Use pre-chopped vegetables to save on prep time.
- If you prefer a thicker soup, you can blend a portion of the soup until smooth and then return it to the pot

Ingredient	Serving Size	Calories	Protein	Carbs	Fiber	Fat	GI	Points per Serving	Servings Used	Total Points
Lentils (cooked)	1 cup	230	18	40	16	1	Low	0	1	0
Chopped Vegetables	1 cup	~50	~2	~10	~3	~0	Low	0	1	0
Vegetable Broth	4 cups	40	1	8	0	0	-	0	1	0
Olive Oil	1 tablespoon	120	0	0	0	14	-	1.2	1	1.2
Dried Thyme, Salt, Pepper	-	~0	~0	~0	~0	~0	-	0	-	0
Total		~440	~21	~58	~19	~15				1.2
Points per Serving									4	0.3

15. Mediterranean Tuna Melt

This comforting and satisfying tuna melt offers a healthy twist on a classic favorite. The whole-wheat bread provides fiber and complex carbohydrates, while the tuna salad filling offers a good source of protein and healthy fats. The addition of Kalamata olives and red onion adds a burst of Mediterranean flavor, and the melted cheese provides a touch of indulgence.

Prep Time: *10 minutes* **Cook Time:** *5 minutes* **Total Time:** *15 minutes* **Servings:** *1*

Ingredients:

- 2 slices whole wheat bread
- 1 can tuna in water, drained
- 2 tablespoons plain non-fat Greek yogurt
- ¼ cup chopped red onion
- ¼ cup chopped Kalamata olives
- 1 slice tomato
- 1 slice low-fat cheese

Alternative ingredients for low budget and allergies:

- **Tuna:** Substitute with canned salmon or cooked, shredded chicken breast
- **Greek Yogurt:** If dairy-free, use a plant-based yogurt alternative
- **Cheese:** If you're watching your points or have dietary restrictions, you can omit the cheese or use a very thin slice

Directions:

1. In a medium bowl, combine the tuna, Greek yogurt, red onion, and Kalamata olives.
2. Season with salt and pepper to taste
3. Spread the tuna salad mixture evenly on one slice of whole-wheat bread
4. Top with the tomato slice and cheese
5. Place the other slice of bread on top
6. Heat a skillet over medium heat and cook the sandwich for 2-3 minutes per side, or until the bread is toasted and the cheese is melted and bubbly

Nutritional facts:

Macronutrients:

  Calories: ~350

  Protein: ~30g

  Carbs: ~35g

  Fiber: ~5g

  Fat: ~12g

Micronutrients:

  Vitamin D: ~20% Daily Value (from tuna)

  Calcium: ~200mg (from cheese and yogurt)

  Iron: ~2mg

  Potassium: ~400mg

Special diet specification and recommendation:

- Easily adaptable for gluten-free diets (use gluten-free bread).
- A great option for a quick and satisfying lunch or light dinner

Chef tips to make it healthier and faster:

- Use a non-stick skillet to cook the sandwich without adding extra oil
- If you prefer a crispier sandwich, you can toast the bread slices before assembling the sandwich
- Add a sprinkle of dried oregano or other herbs to the tuna salad for extra flavor

Recipe Points: 1.7 points

Ingredient	Serving Size	Calories	Protein	Carbs	Fiber	Fat	GI	Points per Serving	Servings Used	Total Points
Whole Wheat Bread	2 slices	160	8	30	4	2	Medium	1.5	1	1.5
Tuna in water (drained)	1 can (5 oz)	120	25	0	0	1	-	0	1	0
Plain non-fat Greek Yogurt	2 tablespoons	33	5.1	2	0	0	Low	0	1	0
Red Onion (chopped)	¼ cup	16	0.4	4	0.6	0	-	0	1	0
Kalamata Olives (chopped)	¼ cup	50	0	1	1	5	-	0	1	0
Tomato (sliced)	1 slice	4	0.2	1	0.2	0	-	0	1	0
Low-fat Cheese	1 slice	45	6	1	0	2	-	0.2	1	0.2
Salt and pepper	To taste	0	0	0	0	0	-	0	-	0
Total		~428	~39.7	~38	~5.8	~10				1.7
Points per Serving									1	1.7

131

Flavorful Dinners for the Whole Family

Baked Salmon with Mediterranean Salsa:

This dish showcases the beauty of simple, fresh ingredients coming together to create a vibrant and nutritious meal. The salmon, rich in omega-3 fatty acids, provides heart-healthy benefits and a good source of protein. The Mediterranean salsa, bursting with colorful vegetables and herbs, adds a refreshing and flavorful counterpoint to the richness of the fish. Baking the salmon ensures it stays moist and tender, while the salsa adds a burst of vibrant flavors.

Prep Time: *15 minutes* **Cook Time:** *12-15 minutes* **Total Time:** *27-30 minutes* **Servings:** 4

Ingredients:

- 4 salmon fillets
- 1 cup chopped tomatoes
- ½ cup chopped cucumber
- ¼ cup chopped red onion
- ¼ cup chopped Kalamata olives
- 2 tablespoons chopped fresh parsley
- 1 tablespoon olive oil
- 1 tablespoon lemon juice
- Salt and pepper to taste

Alternative ingredients for low budget and allergies:

- **Salmon:** You can substitute with another type of fish like cod or tilapia.
- **Kalamata Olives:** If you don't have Kalamata olives, any other type of olive or even capers would work

Directions:

1. Preheat your oven to 400°F (200°C).
2. Season the salmon fillets with salt and pepper
3. In a medium bowl, combine the chopped tomatoes, cucumber, red onion, Kalamata olives, and parsley
4. Add the olive oil and lemon juice to the salsa and toss to coat evenly
5. Place the salmon fillets on a baking sheet lined with parchment paper.
6. Top each salmon fillet with a generous portion of the Mediterranean salsa
7. Bake in the preheated oven for 12-15 minutes, or until the salmon is cooked through and flakes easily with a fork.

Nutritional facts (per serving):

Macronutrients:

Calories: ~300
Protein: ~30g
Carbs: ~15g
Fiber: ~3g
Fat: ~15g

Micronutrients:

Vitamin D: ~50% Daily Value (from salmon)
Calcium: ~50mg
Iron: ~2mg
Potassium: ~600mg

Special diet specification and recommendation:

- Suitable for gluten-free and dairy-free diets.
- A great option for a heart-healthy and satisfying dinner that's easy to prepare.

Chef tips to make it healthier and cook faster:

- To ensure even cooking, choose salmon fillets that are similar in size and thickness
- For a smoky flavor, you can lightly char the vegetables in a grill pan before adding them to the salsa
- Serve with a side of steamed or roasted vegetables for a complete meal

Recipe Points: 0.75 points per serving

Ingredient	Serving Size	Calories	Protein	Carbs	Fiber	Fat	GI	Points per Serving	Servings Used	Total Points
Salmon Fillets	4 (4 oz each)	680	88	0	0	40	Low	0	1	0
Tomatoes (chopped)	1 cup	22	1	5	1	0	Low	0	1	0
Cucumber (chopped)	½ cup	8	0.5	2	0.5	0	-	0	1	0
Red Onion (chopped)	¼ cup	16	0.4	4	0.6	0	-	0	1	0
Kalamata Olives (chopped)	¼ cup	50	0	1	1	5	-	0	1	0
Fresh Parsley (chopped)	2 tablespoons	2	0.2	0.4	0.2	0	-	0	1	0
Olive Oil	1 tablespoon	120	0	0	0	14	-	1.2	1	1.2
Lemon Juice	1 tablespoon	3	0	1	0	0	-	0	1	0
Salt and Pepper	To taste	0	0	0	0	0	-	0	-	0
Total		~901	~90.1	~13	~3.3	~59				1.2
Points per Serving									4	0.3

134

2. Chickpea and Vegetable Tagine

This aromatic and flavorful tagine is a hearty and satisfying vegetarian option that's perfect for a family dinner. The chickpeas provide a good source of plant-based protein and fiber, while the vegetables add a variety of vitamins, minerals, and antioxidants. The blend of warm spices creates a fragrant and inviting dish that's sure to please everyone at the table

Prep Time: *20 minutes* **Cook Time:** *20-25 minutes* **Total Time:** *40-45 minutes* **Servings:** *4*

Ingredients

- 1 tablespoon olive oil
- 1 onion, chopped
- 2 cloves garlic, minced
- 1 teaspoon ground cumin
- ½ teaspoon ground coriander
- ½ teaspoon turmeric
- 1 can (14.5 oz) diced tomatoes
- 1 cup vegetable broth
- 1 can (15 oz) chickpeas, drained and rinsed
- 1 cup chopped mixed vegetables (carrots, bell peppers, zucchini)
- Salt and pepper to taste
- Chopped fresh cilantro for garnish

Alternative ingredients for low budget and allergies:

- If you don't have all the spices on hand, you can use a pre-made curry powder blend
- Feel free to substitute the mixed vegetables with any combination of your favorite vegetables, such as butternut squash, eggplant, or green beans

Directions

1. Heat the olive oil in a large pot or Dutch oven over medium heat
2. Add the chopped onion and cook until softened, about 5 minutes

135

3. Add the minced garlic, ground cumin, coriander, and turmeric. Cook for 1 minute more, stirring constantly
4. Stir in the diced tomatoes, vegetable broth, chickpeas, and mixed vegetables
5. Season with salt and pepper to taste
6. Bring the mixture to a boil, then reduce heat to low, cover, and simmer for 15-20 minutes, or until the vegetables are tender
7. Garnish with chopped fresh cilantro and serve with a side of brown rice or quinoa (consider points if applicable)

Nutritional facts (per serving):

Macronutrients:

Calories: ~300
Protein: ~12g
Carbs: ~45g
Fiber: ~10g
Fat: ~8g

Micronutrients:

Vitamin D: negligible
Calcium: ~60mg
Iron: ~4mg
Potassium: ~600mg

Special diet specification and recommendation:

- Suitable for vegan and gluten-free diets
- A great option for a hearty and flavorful vegetarian meal that's packed with nutrients.

Chef tips to make it healthier and faster:

- Use pre-chopped vegetables to save on prep time
- If you prefer a spicier tagine, add a pinch of cayenne pepper or chopped chili pepper
- Serve with a dollop of plain yogurt for extra creaminess and protein (consider points if applicable)

Recipe Points: 0.3 points per serving

Ingredient	Serving Size	Calories	Protein	Carbs	Fiber	Fat	GI	Points per Serving	Servings Used	Total Points
Olive Oil	1 tablespoon	120	0	0	0	14	-	1.2	1	1.2
Onion (chopped)	1 medium	64	1.5	15	2	0	-	0	1	0
Garlic (minced)	2 cloves	9	0.5	2	0.2	0	-	0	1	0
Spices (cumin, coriander, turmeric)	-	~0	~0	~0	~0	~0	-	0	-	0
Diced Tomatoes (canned)	1 can (14									

3. Lentil Shepherd's Pie:

This hearty and comforting dish is a delightful plant-based twist on a classic comfort food. The lentils, packed with protein and fiber, create a savory and satisfying filling, while the mashed sweet potatoes offer a naturally sweet and creamy topping. The blend of herbs and spices adds warmth and depth, making this a perfect meal for a cozy evening.

Prep Time: *20 minutes* **Cook Time**: *25-30 minutes* **Total Time**: *45-50 minutes* **Servings**: *4*

Ingredients:

- 1 tablespoon olive oil
- 1 onion, chopped
- 2 carrots, chopped
- 2 cloves garlic, minced
- 1 teaspoon dried thyme
- ½ teaspoon dried rosemary
- 1 cup cooked lentils
- 1 cup vegetable broth
- Salt and pepper to taste
- 2 cups mashed sweet potatoes (prepared with no added butter or milk)

Alternative ingredients for low budget and allergies:

- If you don't have sweet potatoes, you can use regular potatoes, but keep in mind they have a slightly higher glycemic index.
- If you prefer a different type of lentil, feel free to substitute with brown or green lentils

Directions:

1. Preheat your oven to 375°F (190°C)
2. Heat the olive oil in a large skillet over medium heat
3. Add the chopped onion and carrots and cook until softened, about 5 minutes.
4. Add the minced garlic, dried thyme, and rosemary. Cook for 1 minute more, stirring frequently
5. Stir in the cooked lentils and vegetable broth
6. Season with salt and pepper to taste

7. Bring the mixture to a simmer and cook for 5-10 minutes, or until the flavors have melded
8. Transfer the lentil mixture to a baking dish
9. Top with the mashed sweet potatoes, spreading them evenly over the lentil mixture.
10. Bake in the preheated oven for 20-25 minutes, or until the sweet potatoes are golden brown and the filling is heated through

Nutritional facts (per serving):

Macronutrients:
Calories: ~350
Protein: ~15g
Carbs: ~50g
Fiber: ~12g
Fat: ~10g

Micronutrients:
Vitamin D: negligible
Calcium: ~50mg
Iron: ~4mg
Potassium: ~600mg

Special diet specification and recommendation:

- Suitable for vegan and gluten-free diets
- A great option for a hearty and comforting plant-based meal that's perfect for the whole family

Chef tips to make it healthier and cook faster:

- Use pre-cooked lentils to save time
- If you don't have fresh herbs, you can use dried herbs, but reduce the amount by half.
- For a richer flavor, you can add a splash of red wine to the lentil mixture while simmering

Ingredient	Serving Size	Calories	Protein	Carbs	Fiber	Fat	GI	Points per Serving	Servings Used	Total Points
Olive Oil	1 tablespoon	120	0	0	0	14	-	1.2	1	1.2
Onion (chopped)	1 medium	64	1.5	15	2	0	-	0	1	0
Carrots (chopped)	2 medium	54	1.2	13	3.6	0.2	Low	0	1	0
Garlic (minced)	2 cloves	9	0.5	2	0.2	0	-	0	1	0
Dried Thyme & Rosemary	-	~0	~0	~0	~0	~0	-	0	-	0
Lentils (cooked)	1 cup	230	18	40	16	1	Low	0	1	0
Vegetable Broth	1 cup	10	0.5	2	0	0	-	0	1	0
Salt and Pepper	To taste	0	0	0	0	0	-	0	-	0
Sweet Potatoes (mashed, no added fat)	2 cups	320	4	70	12	0	Medium	3.5	1	3.5
Total		~ 807	~25.7	~142	~33.8	~15.2				4.7
Points per Serving									4	1.175

140

4. Mediterranean Grilled Chicken Salad:

This vibrant and refreshing salad is a perfect light dinner option, packed with lean protein, healthy fats, and essential nutrients. The grilled chicken provides a satisfying base, while the mixed greens, cucumber, tomatoes, and olives offer a delightful medley of flavors and textures. The crumbled feta cheese adds a touch of creamy saltiness, and the balsamic vinaigrette ties everything together with a tangy and flavorful touch

Prep Time: *20 minutes* **Cook Time:** *10-12 minutes* **Total Time:** *30-32 minutes* **Servings:** 4

Ingredients:

- 4 boneless, skinless chicken breasts
- 1 tablespoon olive oil
- Dried oregano, salt, and pepper to taste
- 4 cups mixed greens
- 1 cup chopped cucumber
- 1 cup cherry tomatoes, halved
- ½ cup Kalamata olives, pitted and halved
- ¼ cup crumbled feta cheese
- Balsamic vinaigrette (made with olive oil, balsamic vinegar, Dijon mustard, garlic, salt, and pepper)

Alternative ingredients for low budget and allergies:

- **Chicken:** Substitute with grilled or baked fish, such as salmon or cod
- **Feta Cheese:** If you're watching your points or have dietary restrictions, you can omit the feta cheese or use a small amount of crumbled goat cheese.
- **Mixed Greens:** Use any combination of your favorite salad greens, such as romaine lettuce, spinach, or arugula.

Directions:

1. Season the chicken breasts with olive oil, dried oregano, salt, and pepper
2. Preheat the grill to medium-high heat
3. Grill the chicken breasts for 5-7 minutes per side or until cooked through. Remove from the grill and let rest for a few minutes, then slice
4. In a large bowl, combine the mixed greens, chopped cucumber, halved cherry tomatoes, Kalamata olives, and crumbled feta cheese.
5. Toss the salad with the balsamic vinaigrette

6. Top the salad with the sliced grilled chicken
7. Serve immediately

Nutritional facts (per serving):

Macronutrients:
      Calories: ~350
      Protein: ~30g
      Carbs: ~20g
      Fiber: ~5g
      Fat: ~18g

Micronutrients:
      Vitamin D: negligible
      Calcium: ~100mg
      Iron: ~3mg
      Potassium: ~500mg

Special diet specification and recommendation:

- Suitable for gluten-free diets
- A great option for a light and protein-packed dinner that's perfect for a warm evening

Chef tips to make it healthier and faster:

- Grill the chicken breasts ahead of time and store them in the refrigerator for quick assembly.
- Make a large batch of balsamic vinaigrette to have on hand for future salads
- Add a handful of chopped nuts or seeds for extra crunch and healthy fats.

Recipe Points: 0.75 points per serving

Ingredient	Serving Size	Calories	Protein	Carbs	Fiber	Fat	GI	Points per Serving	Servings Used	Total Points
Chicken Breast (boneless, skinless)	4 (3 oz each)	560	104	0	0	12	–	0	1	0
Mixed Greens	4 cups	28	4	6	4	0	Low	0	1	0
Cucumber (chopped)	1 cup	16	1	4	1	0	–	0	1	0

5. Shrimp Scampi with Zucchini Noodles:

This light and flavorful dish is a delightful alternative to traditional pasta scampi. The zucchini noodles offer a low-carb, nutrient-rich base, while the succulent shrimp provides a good source of protein. The garlic, white wine, and red pepper flakes create a fragrant and flavorful sauce that perfectly complements the delicate shrimp and zucchini.

Prep Time: *15 minutes* **Cook Time:** *10 minutes* **Total Time:** *25 minutes* **Servings:** *2*

Ingredients

- 1 tablespoon olive oil
- 3 cloves garlic, minced
- ½ teaspoon red pepper flakes
- 1 pound shrimp, peeled and deveined
- ½ cup dry white wine
- 2 zucchini, spiralized into noodles
- ¼ cup chopped fresh parsley
- Salt and pepper to taste

Alternative Ingredients for Low Budget and Allergies:

- **Shrimp:** Substitute with firm tofu cubes or tempeh cubes, marinated in a similar way.
- **Zucchini Noodles:** If you don't have a spiralizer, you can use a vegetable peeler to create long, thin ribbons of zucchini or substitute with spaghetti squash.
- **White Wine:** Substitute with vegetable broth or additional lemon juice for a non-alcoholic version

Directions

1. Heat the olive oil in a large skillet over medium heat.
2. Add the minced garlic and red pepper flakes and cook until fragrant, about 30 seconds
3. Add the shrimp to the skillet and cook until pink and cooked through, about 3-4 minutes per side.
4. Add the white wine to the skillet and bring to a simmer. Cook for 1 minute, or until the liquid has reduced slightly

5. Add the zucchini noodles to the skillet and cook until tender-crisp, about 2-3 minutes
6. Stir in the chopped parsley and season with salt and pepper to taste
7. Serve immediately

Nutritional Facts (per serving):

Macronutrients:
Calories: ~300
Protein: ~30g
Carbs: ~15g
Fiber: ~3g
Fat: ~15g

Micronutrients:
Vitamin D: negligible
Calcium: ~60mg
Iron: ~3mg
Potassium: ~500mg

Special diet specification and recommendation:

- Suitable for gluten-free and low-carb diets
- Can be easily adapted for vegetarian or vegan diets by substituting the shrimp with tofu or tempeh

Chef tips to make it healthier and faster:

- If you don't have a spiralizer, you can use a vegetable peeler to create zucchini ribbons
- For a richer flavor, you can add a squeeze of lemon juice or a pat of butter at the end (consider points if using butter)

Ingredient	Serving Size	Calories	Protein	Carbs	Fiber	Fat	GI	Points per Serving	Servings Used	Total Points
Shrimp (peeled & deveined)	1 pound	500	100	0	0	10	-	0	1	0
Zucchini (spiralized)	2 medium	66	4	12	4	0.8	Low	0	1	0
Olive Oil	1 tablespoon	120	0	0	0	14	-	1.2	1	1.2
Garlic (minced)	3 cloves	13.5	0.6	3	0.3	0	-	0	1	0
Red Pepper Flakes	½ teaspoon	~6	~0	~1	~0	~0	-	0	1	0
Dry White Wine	½ cup	59	0	3	0	0	-	0.3	1	0.3
Fresh Parsley (chopped)	¼ cup	2	0.2	0.4	0.2	0	-	0	1	0
Salt and Pepper	To taste	0	0	0	0	0	-	0	-	0
Total		~760.5	~105	~16.4	~4.5	~28.8				1.5
Points per Serving									2	0.75

6. Vegetable Paella

This vibrant and flavorful paella is a celebration of Mediterranean vegetables and spices. The brown rice provides a hearty and nutritious base, while the colorful vegetables add a variety of vitamins, minerals, and antioxidants. The smoked paprika and saffron infuse the dish with a warm and inviting aroma, making it a perfect centerpiece for a special occasion or a family gathering.

Prep Time: 20 minutes **Cook Time:** 30-35 minutes **Total Time:** 50-55 minutes
Servings: 4

Ingredients:

- 1 tablespoon olive oil
- 1 onion, chopped
- 2 cloves garlic, minced
- 1 teaspoon smoked paprika
- ½ teaspoon saffron threads
- 1 cup brown rice
- 2 cups vegetable broth
- 1 cup chopped mixed vegetables (bell peppers, green beans, peas)
- Salt and pepper to taste
- Chopped fresh parsley for garnish

Alternative ingredients for low budget and allergies

- If saffron is unavailable or too expensive, you can omit it or substitute it with a pinch of turmeric for color
- Feel free to use any combination of vegetables you have on hand, such as chopped tomatoes, artichoke hearts, or asparagus

Directions:

1. Heat the olive oil in a large paella pan or skillet over medium heat
2. Add the chopped onion and cook until softened, about 5 minutes
3. Add the minced garlic and cook for 30 seconds more, until fragrant
4. Stir in the smoked paprika and saffron threads. Cook for another 30 seconds, stirring constantly
5. Add the brown rice to the pan and toast for 1 minute, stirring constantly
6. Pour in the vegetable broth and bring to a boil.

7. Reduce heat to low, cover, and simmer for 15 minutes, or until the rice has absorbed most of the liquid
8. Add the chopped mixed vegetables, cover, and cook for 5-7 minutes more, or until the vegetables are tender-crisp and the rice is cooked through
9. Season with salt and pepper to taste
10. Garnish with chopped fresh parsley and serve immediately

Nutritional Facts (per serving):

Macronutrients

 Calories: ~280

 Protein: ~7g

 Carbs: ~45g

 Fiber: ~5g

 Fat: ~8g

Micronutrients:

 Vitamin D: negligible

 Calcium: ~30mg

 Iron: ~3mg

 Potassium: ~400mg

Special diet specification and recommendation:

- Suitable for vegan and gluten-free diets
- A great option for a flavorful and satisfying vegetarian meal that's perfect for sharing

Chef tips to make it healthier and faster:

- Use pre-cooked brown rice to save time
- If you don't have a paella pan, you can use a large skillet or Dutch oven
- Add a squeeze of lemon juice just before serving for extra brightness

Recipe Points: 0.8 points per serving

Ingredient	Serving Size	Calories	Protein	Carbs	Fiber	Fat	GI	Points per Serving	Servings Used	Total Points
Olive Oil	1 tablespoon	120	0	0	0	14	-	1.2	1	1.2
Onion (chopped)	1 medium	64	1.5	15	2	0	-	0	1	0
Garlic (minced)	2 cloves	9	0.5	2	0.2	0	-	0	1	0
Smoked Paprika & Saffron	-	~0	~0	~0	~0	~0	-	0	-	0
Brown Rice	1 cup	216	4	44	3	2	Medium	2	1	2
Vegetable Broth	2 cups	20	1	4	0	0	-	0	1	0
Mixed Vegetables (chopped)	1 cup	~50	~2	~10	~3	~0	Low	0	1	0
Salt and Pepper	To taste	0	0	0	0	0	-	0	-	0
Fresh Parsley (chopped)	For garnish	~0	~0	~0	~0	~0	-	0	-	0
Total		~679	~8.5	~75	~8.2	~16				3.2
Points per Serving									4	0.8

7. Mediterranean Baked Cod:

This simple yet elegant dish highlights the delicate flavors of cod, enhanced by a zesty Mediterranean crust. The lemon zest and juice add brightness, while the garlic and oregano infuse the fish with warmth and aromatic notes. The cherry tomatoes and Kalamata olives provide a burst of color and additional Mediterranean flair. Baking the cod ensures it stays moist and flaky, making it a perfect choice for a light and healthy dinner

Prep Time: *10 minutes* **Cook Time**: *15-20 minutes* **Total Time**: *25-30 minutes* **Servings**: 4

Ingredients:

- 4 cod fillets
- 1 tablespoon olive oil
- 1 lemon, zested and juiced
- 2 cloves garlic, minced
- ½ teaspoon dried oregano
- Salt and pepper to taste
- 1 cup cherry tomatoes, halved
- ½ cup Kalamata olives, pitted and halved

Alternative Ingredients for Low Budget and Allergies:

- **Cod:** You can substitute with another type of white fish, such as tilapia or haddock.
- **Kalamata Olives:** If you don't have Kalamata olives, you can use any other type of olive or even capers.

Directions:

1. Preheat your oven to 400°F (200°C).
2. Place the cod fillets in a baking dish
3. In a small bowl, combine the olive oil, lemon zest, lemon juice, minced garlic, and dried oregano
4. Drizzle the mixture over the cod fillets, ensuring they are well coated.
5. Season the cod fillets with salt and pepper to taste.
6. Scatter the halved cherry tomatoes and Kalamata olives around the cod fillets in the baking dish

7. Bake in the preheated oven for 15-20 minutes, or until the cod is cooked through and flakes easily with a fork.

Macronutrients:
    Calories: ~250
    Protein: ~30g
    Carbs: ~10g
    Fiber: ~2g
    Fat: ~10g

Micronutrients:
    Vitamin D: ~10% Daily Value
    Calcium: ~40mg
    Iron: ~1mg
    Potassium: ~500mg

Special Diet Specification and Recommendation

- Suitable for gluten-free and dairy-free diets
- A great option for a light and healthy dinner that is rich in omega-3 fatty acids.

Chef tips to make it healthier and cook faster

- For extra flavor, you can add a pinch of red pepper flakes or a sprinkle of chopped fresh herbs like parsley or dill to the lemon-garlic mixture
- Serve with a side of steamed or roasted vegetables for a complete meal.

Ingredient	Serving Size	Calories	Protein	Carbs	Fiber	Fat	GI	Points per Serving	Servings Used	Total Points
Cod Fillets	4 (4 oz each)	320	64	0	0	8	-	0	1	0
Olive Oil	1 tablespoon	120	0	0	0	14	-	1.2	1	1.2
Lemon (zest and juice)	1 medium	20	0.5	5	1.5	0	-	0	1	0
Garlic (minced)	2 cloves	9	0.5	2	0.2	0	-	0	1	0
Dried Oregano	½ teaspoon	2	0.1	0.4	0.2	0.1	-	0	1	0
Salt and Pepper	To taste	0	0	0	0	0	-	0	-	0
Cherry Tomatoes (halved)	1 cup	25	1	6	1.5	0	Low	0	1	0
Kalamata Olives (pitted & halved)	½ cup	100	0	2	2	10	-	0	1	0
Total		~606	~66.1	~15.4	~5.4	~32.1				1.2
Points per Serving									4	0.3

152

8. Stuffed Bell Peppers

These colorful and flavorful stuffed bell peppers are a delightful and nutritious vegetarian meal that's perfect for the whole family. The filling, made with a combination of brown rice, lentils, onions, and mushrooms, is packed with protein, fiber, and essential nutrients. The bell peppers add a burst of color and vitamins, while the simple seasoning of olive oil and oregano enhances the natural flavors of the ingredients.

Prep Time: *20 minutes* **Cook Time**: *30-35 minutes* **Total Time**: *50-55 minutes* **Servings**: 4

Ingredients:

- 4 bell peppers (any color), halved and seeded
- 1 cup cooked brown rice
- 1 cup cooked lentils
- ½ cup chopped onion
- ½ cup chopped mushrooms
- 1 tablespoon olive oil
- ½ teaspoon dried oregano
- Salt and pepper to taste

Alternative Ingredients for Low Budget and Allergies:

- **Bell Peppers:** If bell peppers are unavailable or cause allergies, you can use large portobello mushroom caps as a substitute.
- **Brown Rice:** You can substitute with another cooked whole grain like quinoa or barley

Directions:

1. Preheat your oven to 375°F (190°C).
2. Heat the olive oil in a large skillet over medium heat
3. Add the chopped onion and mushrooms and sauté until softened, about 5 minutes
4. In a large bowl, combine the cooked brown rice, cooked lentils, sautéed onion and mushrooms, and dried oregano
5. Season with salt and pepper to taste

6. Fill the halved bell peppers with the rice and lentil mixture, dividing it equally among them
7. Place the stuffed peppers in a baking dish and add a small amount of water to the bottom of the dish to create steam.
8. Bake in the preheated oven for 25-30 minutes, or until the peppers are tender and the filling is heated through

Nutritional Facts (per serving):

Macronutrients:

Calories: ~300

Protein: ~12g

Carbs: ~45g

Fiber: ~8g

Fat: ~8g

Micronutrients:

Vitamin D: negligible

Calcium: ~40mg

Iron: ~4mg

Potassium: ~500mg

Special diet specification and recommendation:

- Suitable for vegan and gluten-free diets
- A great option for a hearty and satisfying vegetarian meal that is packed with nutrients

Chef tips to make it healthier and faster

- Use pre-cooked brown rice and lentils to save time
- If you prefer a cheesier filling, you can sprinkle a small amount of crumbled feta or goat cheese on top of the stuffed peppers before baking (consider points if using).
- Serve with a side salad or a dollop of plain yogurt for a complete meal.

Ingredient	Serving Size	Calories	Protein	Carbs	Fiber	Fat	GI	Points per Serving	Servings Used	Total Points
Bell Peppers (halved & seeded)	4	120	4	28	8	0	Low	0	1	0
Brown Rice (cooked)	1 cup	216	4	44	3	2	Medium	2	1	2
Lentils (cooked)	1 cup	230	18	40	16	1	Low	0	1	0
Onion (chopped)	½ cup	32	0.8	8	1.2	0	-	0	1	0
Mushrooms (chopped)	½ cup	10	1.5	2	1	0	-	0	1	0
Olive Oil	1 tablespoon	120	0	0	0	14	-	1.2	1	1.2
Dried Oregano	½ teaspoon	2	0.1	0.4	0.2	0.1	-	0	1	0
Salt and Pepper	To taste	0	0	0	0	0	-	0	-	0
Total		~740	~28.4	~122.4	~29.4	~17.1				3.2
Points per Serving									4	0.8

9. Greek Salad with Grilled Chicken

This refreshing and vibrant salad is a classic Mediterranean dish that's perfect for a light and satisfying dinner. The combination of crisp greens, juicy tomatoes, cucumbers, Kalamata olives, and feta cheese offers a delightful medley of flavors and textures. The grilled chicken adds a lean protein boost, while the red wine vinaigrette ties everything together with a tangy and flavorful touch.

Prep Time: *20 minutes* **Cook Time**: *10-12 minutes* **Total Time**: *30-32 minutes* **Servings**: 4

Ingredients:

- 4 cups mixed greens
- 1 cup chopped cucumber
- 1 cup cherry tomatoes, halved
- ½ cup Kalamata olives, pitted and halved
- ¼ cup crumbled feta cheese
- 4 oz grilled chicken breast, sliced
- Red wine vinaigrette (made with olive oil, red wine vinegar, Dijon mustard, garlic, salt, and pepper)

Alternative ingredients for low budget and allergies:

- **Chicken:** Substitute with grilled or baked fish, such as salmon or cod.
- **Feta Cheese:** If you're watching your points or have dietary restrictions, you can omit the feta cheese or use a small amount of crumbled goat cheese.
- **Mixed Greens:** Use any combination of your favorite salad greens, such as romaine lettuce, spinach, or arugula.

Directions:

1. Season the chicken breast with salt and pepper and grill over medium heat for 5-7 minutes per side or until cooked through. Remove from the grill and let rest for a few minutes, then slice
2. In a large bowl, combine the mixed greens, chopped cucumber, halved cherry tomatoes, Kalamata olives, and crumbled feta cheese
3. In a small bowl, whisk together the olive oil, red wine vinegar, Dijon mustard, minced garlic, salt, and pepper to make the vinaigrette
4. Pour the vinaigrette over the salad and toss to coat evenly.
5. Top the salad with the sliced grilled chicken.

6. Serve immediately

Macronutrients:

    Calories: ~250

    Protein: ~20g

    Carbs: ~12g

    Fiber: ~4g

    Fat: ~15g

Micronutrients:

    Vitamin D: negligible

    Calcium: ~80mg

    Iron: ~2mg

    Potassium: ~400mg

Special diet specification and recommendation:

- Suitable for gluten-free diets
- A great option for a light and protein-packed dinner that's perfect for a warm evening

Chef tips to make it healthier and faster:

- Grill the chicken breasts ahead of time and store them in the refrigerator for quick assembly
- Make a large batch of red wine vinaigrette to have on hand for future salads
- Add a handful of chopped nuts or seeds for extra crunch and healthy fats

Recipe Points: 0.6 points per serving

Ingredient	Serving Size	Calories	Protein	Carbs	Fiber	Fat	GI	Points per Serving	Servings Used	Total Points
Chicken Breast (boneless, skinless)	4 (3 oz each)	560	104	0	0	12	-	0	1	0
Mixed Greens	4 cups	28	4	6	4	0	Low	0	1	0
Cucumber (chopped)	1 cup	16	1	4	1	0	-	0	1	0
Cherry Tomatoes (halved)	1 cup	25	1	6	1.5	0	Low	0	1	0
Kalamata Olives (pitted & halved)	½ cup	100	0	2	2	10	-	0	1	0
Feta Cheese (crumbled)	¼ cup	100	6	4	0	8	-	1	1	1
Red Wine Vinaigrette	(let's assume 2 tbsp total)	120	0	3	0	13	-	1.3	1	1.3
Salt and Pepper	To taste	0	0	0	0	0	-	0	-	0
Total		~949	~116	~25	~8.5	~33				2.3
Points per Serving									4	0.575

158

10. Mediterranean Chickpea Burgers:

These flavorful and hearty chickpea burgers are a delightful vegetarian option that is packed with protein and fiber. The combination of chickpeas, onion, parsley, and spices creates a delicious and satisfying patty that's perfect for grilling or pan-frying. Served on whole-wheat buns with lettuce, tomato, and hummus, these burgers are a healthy and fulfilling meal for the whole family.

Prep Time: 20 minutes **Cook Time:** 10-12 minutes **Total Time:** 30-32 minutes **Servings:** 4

Ingredients:

- 1 can (15 oz) chickpeas, drained and rinsed
- ½ cup chopped onion
- ¼ cup chopped fresh parsley
- 1 egg
- ½ cup whole wheat breadcrumbs
- Salt and pepper to taste
- Olive oil for cooking
- Whole wheat buns
- Lettuce, tomato slices, and hummus for serving

Alternative Ingredients for Low Budget and Allergies

- **Chickpeas:** Substitute with another type of bean, such as black beans or kidney beans
- **Egg:** For a vegan option, use a flax egg (1 tablespoon ground flaxseed mixed with 3 tablespoons water) or mashed avocado as a binder.
- **Whole Wheat Breadcrumbs:** Substitute with almond flour or oat flour for a gluten-free option

Directions:

1. In a large bowl, mash the chickpeas with a fork or potato masher until mostly smooth, leaving some texture.
2. Add the chopped onion, parsley, egg, breadcrumbs, salt, and pepper to the bowl. Mix well until all the ingredients are combined
3. Form the mixture into 4 patties
4. Heat a drizzle of olive oil in a large skillet over medium heat

5. Carefully place the patties in the hot skillet and cook for about 5-6 minutes per side, or until golden brown and heated through
6. Serve on whole-wheat buns with lettuce, tomato slices, and hummus.

Nutritional Facts (per serving):

Macronutrients:
　　Calories: ~350 (without bun and toppings)
　　Protein: ~15g
　　Carbs: ~40g
　　Fiber: ~8g
　　Fat: ~12g

Micronutrients:
　　Vitamin D: negligible
　　Calcium: ~50mg
　　Iron: ~3mg
　　Potassium: ~400mg

Special diet specification and recommendation:

- Can be easily adapted for vegan and gluten-free diets (with substitutions mentioned above)
- A great option for a hearty and satisfying vegetarian meal.

Chef tips to make it healthier and cook faster:

- If the mixture is too wet, add a bit more breadcrumbs to help it hold its shape.
- You can also bake the patties in a preheated oven at 375°F for about 20-25 minutes, flipping halfway through, for a healthier option.
- Serve with a side salad or roasted vegetables for a complete meal

Recipe Points: 0.7 points per serving (without bun and toppings)

Ingredient	Serving Size	Calories	Protein	Carbs	Fiber	Fat	GI	Points per Serving	Servings Used	Total Points
Chickpeas (cooked)	1 can (15 oz)	350	20	62	15	3.5	Low	0	1	0
Onion (chopped)	½ cup	32	0.8	8	1.2	0	–	0	1	0
Fresh Parsley (chopped)	¼ cup	2	0.2	0.4	0.2	0	–	0	1	0
Egg	1 large	70	6	0	0	5	–	0.5	1	0.5
Whole Wheat Breadcrumbs	½ cup	160	6	28	3	1	Medium	1.5	1	1.5
Salt and pepper	To taste	0	0	0	0	0	–	0	–	0
Olive Oil	For cooking (let's assume 2 tablespoons total)	240	0	0	0	28	–	2.8	1	2.8
Total		~854	~33	~98.4	~19.4	~37.5				4.8
Points per Serving (patty only)									4	1.2

11. One-Pan Roasted Chicken and Vegetables

This simple and satisfying one-pan dish is a perfect weeknight meal that's packed with flavor and nutrients. The chicken provides lean protein, while the colorful vegetables offer a variety of vitamins, minerals, and fiber. The combination of olive oil and oregano creates a warm and aromatic flavor profile, making this a delicious and healthy meal that's ready in under 30 minutes

Prep Time: 15 minutes **Cook Time:** 20-25 minutes **Total Time:** 35-40 minutes **Servings:** 4

Ingredients:

- 1 pound boneless, skinless chicken breasts, cut into bite-sized pieces
- 1 tablespoon olive oil
- 1 teaspoon dried oregano
- Salt and pepper to taste
- 1 cup broccoli florets
- 1 cup Brussels sprouts, halved
- 1 cup chopped sweet potatoes

Alternative ingredients for low budget and allergies:

- **Chicken:** Substitute with firm tofu cubes or tempeh cubes, marinated in the same way
- **Vegetables:** Use any combination of your favorite roasting vegetables, such as carrots, parsnips, or cauliflower

Directions:

1. Preheat your oven to 400°F
2. In a large bowl, toss the chicken pieces with olive oil, dried oregano, salt, and pepper until well coated
3. Add the broccoli florets, halved Brussels sprouts, and chopped sweet potatoes to the bowl and toss to combine with the chicken and marinade
4. Spread the chicken and vegetables in a single layer on a large baking sheet lined with parchment paper
5. Roast in the preheated oven for 20-25 minutes, or until the chicken is cooked through and the vegetables are tender

Macronutrients:

      Calories: ~300

      Protein: ~30g

      Carbs: ~25g

      Fiber: ~5g

      Fat: ~10g

Micronutrients:

      Vitamin D: negligible

      Calcium: ~50mg

      Iron: ~2mg

      Potassium: ~500mg

Special diet specification and recommendation

- Suitable for gluten-free and dairy-free diets
- Can be easily adapted for vegetarian or vegan diets by substituting the chicken with tofu or tempeh

Chef tips to make it healthier and faster:

- Cut the vegetables into uniform sizes to ensure even cooking
- If you prefer a crispier texture, you can broil the chicken and vegetables for the last few minutes of cooking

Recipe Points: 0.3 points per serving

Ingredient	Serving Size	Calories	Protein	Carbs	Fiber	Fat	GI	Points per Serving	Servings Used	Total Points
Chicken Breast (boneless, skinless)	1 pound	560	104	0	0	12	-	0	1	0
Broccoli Florets	1 cup	31	3	6	2.5	0.4	Low	0	1	0
Brussels Sprouts (halved)	1 cup	38	3	7	3	0.3	Low	0	1	0
Sweet Potatoes (chopped)	1 cup	114	2	26	4	0.2	Medium	1.4	1	1.4
Olive Oil	1 tablespoon	120	0	0	0	14	-	1.2		

12. Mediterranean Tuna Pasta Salad

This light and refreshing pasta salad is a perfect lunch or dinner option that's packed with Mediterranean flavors. The whole wheat pasta provides a healthy dose of fiber and complex carbohydrates, while the tuna adds lean protein and omega-3 fatty acids. The colorful vegetables and olives bring a burst of freshness and antioxidants, and the lemon vinaigrette adds a zesty touch. It's a simple yet satisfying dish that's easy to make and perfect for a warm day.

Prep Time: 15 minutes **Cook Time:** 10-12 minutes (for cooking pasta) **Total Time:** 25-27 minutes **Servings:** 4

Ingredients:

- 1 cup cooked whole wheat pasta
- 1 can tuna in water, drained
- ½ cup chopped cucumber
- ½ cup cherry tomatoes, halved
- ¼ cup chopped Kalamata olives
- ¼ cup chopped red onion
- 2 tablespoons chopped fresh parsley
- 2 tablespoons olive oil
- 1 tablespoon lemon juice
- Salt and pepper to taste

Alternative Ingredients for Low Budget and Allergies:

- **Whole Wheat Pasta:** Substitute with gluten-free pasta or another cooked whole grain like quinoa or brown rice.
- **Tuna:** Substitute with canned salmon or cooked, shredded chicken breast.
- **Kalamata Olives:** If you don't have Kalamata olives, any other type of olive or even capers would work

Directions:

1. Cook the whole wheat pasta according to package directions. Drain and set aside to cool slightly
2. In a large bowl, combine the cooked pasta, tuna, cucumber, cherry tomatoes, Kalamata olives, red onion, and parsley

3. In a small bowl, whisk together the olive oil, lemon juice, salt, and pepper to make the vinaigrette
4. Pour the vinaigrette over the pasta salad and toss to coat evenly
5. Serve chilled or at room temperature

Nutritional Facts (per serving):

Macronutrients:

Calories: ~300

Protein: ~20g

Carbs: ~35g

Fiber: ~5g

Fat: ~10g

Micronutrients:

Vitamin D: ~10% Daily Value (from tuna)

Calcium: ~40mg

Iron: ~2mg

Potassium: ~400mg

Special diet specification and recommendation:

- Easily adaptable for gluten-free diets (use gluten-free pasta)
- A great option for a light and refreshing lunch or dinner, packed with protein and healthy fats

Chef tips to make it healthier and faster:

- Cook the pasta al dente for a lower glycemic index
- Add a pinch of red pepper flakes or a dash of hot sauce for a touch of spice
- If you prefer a creamier dressing, you can whisk in a tablespoon of plain non-fat Greek yogurt to the vinaigrette.

Recipe Points: 1.1 points per serving

Ingredient	Serving Size	Calories	Protein	Carbs	Fiber	Fat	GI	Points per Serving	Servings Used	Total Points
Whole Wheat Pasta (cooked)	1 cup	174	7	37	6.3	1.3	Medium	2.5	1	2.5
Tuna in water (drained)	1 can (5 oz)	120	25	0	0	1	-	0	1	0
Cucumber (chopped)	½ cup	8	0.5	2	0.5	0	-	0	1	0
Cherry Tomatoes (halved)	½ cup	15	1	3	1	0	Low	0	1	0
Kalamata Olives (chopped)	¼ cup	50	0	1	1	5	-	0	1	0
Red Onion (chopped)	¼ cup	16	0.4	4	0.6	0	-	0	1	0
Fresh Parsley (chopped)	2 tablespoons	2	0.2	0.4	0.2	0	-	0	1	0
Olive Oil	2 tablespoons	240	0	0	0	28	-	2.8	1	2.8

Lemon Juice	1 tablespoon	3	0	1	0	0	-	0	1	0
Salt and pepper	To taste	0	0	0	0	0	-	0	-	0
Total		~628	~34.1	~48.4	~9.6	~35.3				5.3
Points per Serving									4	1.325

13. Baked Falafel with Tahini Sauce and Salad

These flavorful baked falafel are a delightful vegetarian option, packed with protein and fiber from the chickpeas. The blend of herbs and spices creates a warm and aromatic flavor profile, while baking them instead of frying keeps them light and healthy. Served with a creamy tahini sauce and a refreshing salad, this dish is perfect for a special occasion or a satisfying weeknight meal.

Prep Time: 30 minutes **Cook Time:** 20-25 minutes **Total Time:** 50-55 minutes **Servings:** 4

Ingredients

- 1 can (15oz) chickpeas, drained and rinsed
- ½ cup chopped onion
- ¼ cup chopped fresh parsley
- 2 cloves garlic, minced
- 1 teaspoon ground cumin
- ½ teaspoon ground coriander
- Salt and pepper to taste
- Olive oil for drizzling
- Tahini sauce (made with tahini, lemon juice, garlic, and water)
- Mixed greens salad

Alternative ingredients for low budget and allergies

- If you don't have tahini, you can substitute it with hummus or another bean dip made with zero-point ingredients
- For those with nut allergies, ensure the tahini sauce is made with sesame seeds only and does not contain any nuts

Directions:

1. Preheat oven to 400F.
2. In a food processor, combine the chickpeas, onion, parsley, garlic, cumin, coriander, salt, and pepper. Pulse until coarsely ground, but not completely smooth.
3. Form the mixture into small patties or balls
4. Place the falafel on a baking sheet lined with parchment paper.
5. Drizzle lightly with olive oil.

6. Bake for 20-25 minutes, or until golden brown and slightly crispy on the outside
7. While the falafel is baking, prepare the tahini sauce by whisking together tahini, lemon juice, minced garlic, and water until smooth and creamy
8. Assemble the mixed greens salad with your favorite vegetables
9. Serve the baked falafel with the tahini sauce and a side salad.

Nutritional Facts (per serving):

Macronutrients:
Calories: ~350 (without salad)
Protein: ~15g
Carbs: ~40g
Fiber: ~10g
Fat: ~15g

Micronutrients:
Vitamin D: negligible
Calcium: ~60mg
Iron: ~4mg
Potassium: ~500mg

Special diet specification and recommendation:

- Suitable for vegan and gluten-free diets
- A great option for a protein-rich and flavorful vegetarian meal

Chef tips to make it healthier and faster:

- If you don't have a food processor, you can mash the chickpeas with a fork or potato masher until mostly smooth.
- You can also pan-fry the falafel in a small amount of olive oil for a crispier exterior, but be mindful of the additional fat and points
- Serve with a side of whole-wheat pita bread or brown rice (consider points if applicable)

Recipe Points: 0.3 points per serving (without salad)

Ingredient	Serving Size	Calories	Protein	Carbs	Fiber	Fat	GI	Points per Serving	Servings Used	Total Points
Chickpeas (cooked)	1 can (15 oz)	350	20	62	15	3.5	Low	0	1	0
Onion (chopped)	½ cup	32	0.8	8	1.2	0	-	0	1	0
Fresh Parsley (chopped)	¼ cup	2	0.2	0.4	0.2	0	-	0	1	0
Garlic (minced)	2 cloves	9	0.5	2	0.2	0	-	0	1	0
Spices (cumin, coriander)	-	~0	~0	~0	~0	~0	-	0	-	0
Salt and Pepper	To taste	0	0	0	0	0	-	0	-	0
Olive Oil	For drizzling (let's assume 1 tablespoons total)	120	0	0	0	14	-	1.2	1	1.2
Tahini Sauce	(zero-point)	~100	~3	~5	~2	~9	-	0	-	0

Mixed Greens Salad	–	~0	~0	~0	~0	~0	–	0	–	0
Total		~613	~24.5	~77.4	~18.6	~26.5				1.2
Points per Serving (falafel only)									4	0.3

14. Mediterranean Vegetable Skewers with Tzatziki

These vibrant and flavorful skewers are a delightful and healthy option, perfect for a light dinner or a special occasion appetizer. The colorful vegetables, grilled to perfection, offer a variety of textures and nutrients. The creamy and refreshing tzatziki sauce, made with Greek yogurt, cucumber, and herbs, complements the grilled vegetables beautifully, creating a harmonious and satisfying dish.

Prep Time: 20 minutes **Cook Time:** 10-12 minutes **Total Time:** 30-32 minutes **Servings:** 4

Ingredients:

- 1 zucchini, cut into chunks
- 1 bell pepper, cut into chunks
- 1 red onion, cut into chunks
- 1 cup cherry tomatoes
- 1 tablespoon olive oil
- Dried oregano, salt, and pepper to taste
- Tzatziki sauce (made with plain non-fat Greek yogurt, cucumber, garlic, dill, lemon juice, and salt)

Alternative ingredients for low budget and allergies

- Feel free to use any combination of your favorite vegetables, such as mushrooms, eggplant, or yellow squash.
- If you don't have fresh dill for the tzatziki, you can substitute it with dried dill or another fresh herb like parsley or mint

Directions:

1. Thread the zucchini chunks, bell pepper chunks, red onion chunks, and cherry tomatoes onto skewers, alternating between the ingredients
2. In a small bowl, whisk together the olive oil, dried oregano, salt, and pepper to make the marinade
3. Brush the skewers generously with the marinade.
4. Preheat the grill to medium-high heat

5. Place the skewers on the grill and cook for 10-12 minutes, or until the vegetables are tender-crisp and slightly charred, turning occasionally
6. While the skewers are grilling, prepare the tzatziki sauce.
7. Serve the grilled skewers with a generous dollop of tzatziki sauce.

Nutritional facts (per serving):

Macronutrients:

Calories: ~150 (without tzatziki)
Protein: ~3g
Carbs: ~20g
Fiber: ~4g
Fat: ~7g

Micronutrients:

Vitamin D: negligible
Calcium: ~30mg
Iron: ~1mg
Potassium: ~400mg

Special diet specification and recommendation:

- Suitable for vegan and gluten-free diets.
- A great option for a light and refreshing vegetarian meal or appetizer.

Chef tips to make it healthier and faster:

- Soak the skewers in water for 30 minutes before assembling to prevent them from burning on the grill.
- Marinate the vegetables for at least 30 minutes, or up to overnight, for maximum flavor.
- Make a large batch of tzatziki sauce to have on hand for future meals or snacks

Recipe Points: 0.3 points per serving (without tzatziki)

Ingredient	Serving Size	Calories	Protein	Carbs	Fiber	Fat	GI	Points per Serving	Servings Used	Total Points
Zucchini (chunks)	1 medium	33	2	6	2	0.4	Low	0	1	0
Bell Pepper (chunks)	1 medium	30	1	7	2	0	Low	0	1	0
Red Onion (chunks)	1 medium	64	1.5	15	2	0	-	0	1	0
Cherry Tomatoes	1 cup	25	1	6	1.5	0	Low	0	1	0
Olive Oil	1 tablespoon	120	0	0	0	14	-	1.2	1	1.2
Dried Oregano, Salt, Pepper	-	~0	~0	~0	~0	~0	-	0	-	0
Tzatziki Sauce	(zero-point)	~50	~5	~3	~0	~3	-	0	-	0
Total		~322	~5.5	~37	~6.5	~17.4				1.2
Points per Serving (skewers only)									4	0.3

15. White Bean and Spinach Stew

This hearty and comforting stew is a perfect vegetarian option for a cozy dinner. Cannellini beans, rich in protein and fiber, create a satisfying base, while the spinach adds a boost of vitamins and minerals. The simple combination of olive oil, garlic, oregano, and red pepper flakes creates a warm and flavorful broth that's both nourishing and delicious.

Prep Time: *10 minutes* **Cook Time**: *15-20 minutes* **Total Time**: *25-30 minutes* **Servings**: 4

Ingredients:

- 1 tablespoon olive oil
- 1 onion, chopped
- 2 cloves garlic, minced
- 1 teaspoon dried oregano
- ½ teaspoon red pepper flakes
- 1 can (15 oz) cannellini beans, drained and rinsed
- 4 cups vegetable broth
- 1 bunch spinach, roughly chopped
- Salt and pepper to taste

Alternative Ingredients for Low Budget and Allergies:

- **Cannellini Beans:** Substitute with any other white bean variety, such as Great Northern beans or navy beans.
- **Spinach:** Substitute with another leafy green like kale or Swiss chard

Directions:

1. Heat the olive oil in a large pot over medium heat
2. Add the chopped onion and cook until softened, about 5 minutes
3. Add the minced garlic, dried oregano, and red pepper flakes. Cook for 1 minute more, stirring constantly
4. Stir in the cannellini beans, vegetable broth, and spinach
5. Season with salt and pepper to taste
6. Bring the mixture to a boil, then reduce heat to low and simmer for 10-15 minutes, or until the spinach is wilted and the flavors have melded

Nutritional Facts (per serving):

Macronutrients:

    Calories: ~250

    Protein: ~12g

    Carbs: ~35g

    Fiber: ~10g

    Fat: ~7g

Micronutrients:

    Vitamin D: negligible

    Calcium: ~80mg

    Iron: ~3mg

    Potassium: ~500mg

Special diet specification and recommendation:

- Suitable for vegan and gluten-free diets
- A great option for a hearty and satisfying vegetarian meal that's perfect for a cold evening

Chef tips to make it healthier and faster

- If you prefer a thicker stew, you can mash some of the beans with a fork or potato masher before adding them to the pot
- Add a squeeze of lemon juice just before serving for extra brightness
- Serve with a side of whole-wheat bread or a dollop of plain yogurt for a complete meal (consider points if applicable)

Ingredient	Serving Size	Calories	Protein	Carbs	Fiber	Fat	GI	Points per Serving	Servings Used	Total Points
Olive Oil	1 tablespoon	120	0	0	0	14	-	1.2	1	1.2
Onion (chopped)	1 medium	64	1.5	15	2	0	-	0	1	0
Garlic (minced)	2 cloves	9	0.5	2	0.2	0	-	0	1	0
Dried Oregano & Red Pepper Flakes	-	~0	~0	~0	~0	~0	-	0	-	0
Cannellini Beans (cooked)	1 can (15 oz)	350	20	62	15	3.5	Low	0	1	0
Vegetable Broth	4 cups	40	1	8	0	0	-	0	1	0
Spinach (chopped)	1 bunch (~5 cups)	35	5	7	4	0.5	Low	0	1	0
Salt and Pepper	To taste	0	0	0	0	0	-	0	-	0
Total		~ 618	~28	~94	~21.2	~17.5				1.2
Points per Serving									4	0.3

Healthy Snacks and Sweet Treats

Mediterranean Snacks & Sweet Treats

Ants on a Log

This classic childhood snack is a simple yet satisfying treat that's perfect for any time of day. The celery sticks provide a refreshing crunch and hydration, while the nut butter offers a dose of protein and healthy fats. The raisins add natural sweetness and a touch of antioxidants. It's a fun and easy snack that's both nutritious and delicious.

Prep Time: 5 minutes **Cook Time:** None **Total Time:** 5 minutes **Servings:** 1-2

Ingredients:

- 2-3 celery stalks, washed and cut into 3-inch pieces
- 2 tablespoons natural peanut butter or almond butter
- Raisins or other dried fruit (check for added sugar)

Alternative Ingredients for Low Budget and Allergies:

- **Nut Butter:** If you have a nut allergy, substitute with sunflower seed butter or tahini.
- **Raisins:** Use other dried fruits like cranberries, chopped dates, or dried apricots (ensure no added sugar).

Directions:

1. Spread 1 tablespoon of nut butter into each celery stalk.
2. Arrange raisins along the length of the nut butter.
3. Enjoy immediately!

Nutritional Facts (per serving, assuming 3 celery stalks and 2 tablespoons nut butter):

Macronutrients:
      Calories: ~250
      Protein: ~10g
      Carbs: ~25g
      Fiber: ~5g
      Fat: ~15g

Micronutrients:
      Vitamin D: negligible
      Calcium: ~30mg
      Iron: ~1mg
      Potassium: ~300mg

Special Diet Specification and Recommendation:

- Suitable for vegetarian and gluten-free diets.
- Make sure to choose dried fruits without added sugar.
- If using a nut-free butter, it's suitable for those with nut allergies

Chef Tips to Make it Healthier and Faster:

- Prep the celery sticks ahead of time and store them in an airtight container in the refrigerator for a grab-and-go snack
- You can also use other vegetables like cucumber slices or bell pepper strips as a base
- Get creative with the toppings! Try chopped nuts, seeds, or even a sprinkle of cinnamon

Recipe Points: 0.5 points per serving

Ingredient	Serving Size	Calories	Protein	Carbs	Fiber	Fat	GI	Points per Serving	Servings Used	Total Points
Celery Stalks	3	18	0.9	3	1.8	0.18	Low	0	1	0
Almond Butter	2 tablespoons	190	7	6	3	16	–	1	1	1
Raisins	2 tablespoons	50	1	13	1	0	Medium	0.5	1	0.5
Total		~258	~8.9	~22	~5.8	~16.18				1.5
Points per Serving									1-2	1.5 (1 serving) or 0.75 (2 servings)

2. Greek Yogurt with Berries and Nuts:

This simple and satisfying snack or breakfast is a powerhouse of nutrients. The Greek yogurt provides a creamy texture and a hefty dose of protein, crucial for satiety and muscle maintenance. The mixed berries offer a burst of antioxidants and natural sweetness, while the chopped nuts add healthy fats and a satisfying crunch.

Prep Time: 5 minutes **Cook Time**: None **Total Time**: 5 minutes **Servings**: 1

Ingredients:

- 1 cup plain non-fat Greek yogurt
- ½ cup mixed berries
- 1 tablespoon chopped walnuts or almonds

Alternative Ingredients for Low Budget and Allergies:

- **Greek Yogurt:** If you don't have Greek yogurt, any plain non-fat yogurt will work
- **Berries:** Use any combination of fresh or frozen berries you enjoy.
- **Nuts:** Substitute with seeds (pumpkin, sunflower) if you have nut allergies.

Directions:

1. In a bowl, combine the Greek yogurt, mixed berries, and chopped nuts.
2. Enjoy immediately or store in the refrigerator for later

Nutritional Facts:

Macronutrients:

Calories: ~200
Protein: ~20g
Carbs: ~20g
Fiber: ~4g
Fat: ~7g

Micronutrients:

Vitamin D: negligible (unless yogurt is fortified)
Calcium: ~200mg (from yogurt)
Iron: ~1mg
Potassium: ~400mg

Special diet specification and recommendation:

- Suitable for vegetarian diets
- For a vegan option, use a plant-based yogurt alternative

Chef tips to make it healthier and faster:

- Prep individual servings in jars or containers ahead of time for a grab-and-go snack
- Add a drizzle of honey or a sprinkle of cinnamon for extra sweetness (consider points if applicable)
- If you prefer a thicker yogurt, strain the Greek yogurt in a cheesecloth-lined sieve for a few hours to remove excess liquid

Recipe Points: 0 points (all ingredients are from the no-point food list)

Ingredient	Serving Size	Calories	Protein	Carbs	Fiber	Fat	GI	Points per Serving	Servings Used	Total Points
Plain Non-Fat Greek Yogurt	1 cup	100	17	6	0	0	Low	0	1	0
Mixed Berries	½ cup	31	0.5	7	2	0.25	Low	0	1	0
Walnuts/ Almonds (chopped)	1 tablespoon	45	1	2	1	4	-	0	1	0
Total		~176	~18.5	~15	~3	~4.25				0
Points per Serving									1	0

3. Fruit and Cheese Plate

This simple yet elegant snack or light lunch offers a delightful combination of sweet and savory flavors. The variety of fruits provides essential vitamins, minerals, and antioxidants, while the low-fat cheese adds protein and calcium. It's a perfect option for entertaining or a quick and easy snack when you're on the go.

Prep Time: *10 minutes* **Cook Time**: *None* **Total Time**: *10 minutes* **Servings**: *Varies*

Ingredients:

- Assorted sliced fruits (apples, pears, grapes)
- Cubes of low-fat cheese (feta, mozzarella)

Alternative Ingredients for Low Budget and Allergies:

- **Fruits:** Use any combination of seasonal fruits that you enjoy.
- **Cheese:** If you're watching your points or have dietary restrictions, you can omit the cheese or use a smaller amount.

Directions:

1. Wash and slice the fruits.
2. Cut the cheese into bite-sized cubes
3. Arrange the fruits and cheese on a plate or platter
4. Enjoy!

Nutritional Facts (per serving):

- Will vary depending on the specific fruits and cheese chosen and the portion size. Refer to individual nutritional information for each item

Special diet specification and recommendation: Suitable for vegetarian diets

- If omitting the cheese, this plate is also suitable for vegan and dairy-free diets

Chef tips to make it healthier and faster:

- Prep the fruits and cheese ahead of time and store them in airtight containers in the refrigerator for quick assembly
- Add a handful of nuts or seeds for extra protein and healthy fats (consider points if applicable)

4. Homemade Trail Mix

This customizable trail mix is a powerhouse of nutrients, offering a blend of healthy fats, protein, and antioxidants. The combination of almonds, walnuts, dried fruit, and pumpkin seeds creates a satisfying and flavorful snack that's perfect for on-the-go energy or a midday pick-me-up.

Prep Time: 5 minutes **Cook Time:** None **Total Time:** 5 minutes **Servings:** 4

Ingredients:

- ¼ cup raw almonds
- ¼ cup raw walnuts
- ¼ cup dried cranberries or cherries (no added sugar)
- ¼ cup pumpkin seeds

Alternative ingredients for low budget and allergies:

- **Nuts:** Substitute with any other raw, unsalted nuts or seeds like cashews, pecans, or sunflower seeds
- **Dried Fruit:** Use any other unsweetened dried fruit like chopped dates or apricots

Directions:

1. In a medium bowl, combine all the ingredients.
2. Mix well to ensure even distribution.
3. Divide into individual portions and store in airtight containers for easy snacking on the go.

Nutritional Facts (per serving):

Macronutrients:
Calories: ~200
Protein: ~7g
Carbs: ~15g
Fiber: ~4g
Fat: ~15g

Micronutrients:
Vitamin D: negligible

Calcium: ~50mg

Iron: ~2mg

Potassium: ~250mg

Special diet specification and recommendation:

- Suitable for vegan and gluten-free diets.
- Make sure to choose unsweetened dried fruits

Chef Tips to Make it Healthier and Faster:

- You can roast the nuts lightly for added flavor and crunch
- Add a pinch of cinnamon or other spices for extra warmth and depth

Recipe Points: 0.4 points per serving

Ingredient	Serving Size	Calories	Protein	Carbs	Fiber	Fat	GI	Points per Serving	Servings Used	Total Points
Raw Almonds	¼ cup	207	7	8	4	18	-	0	1	0
Raw Walnuts	¼ cup	185	4	4	2	18	-	0	1	0
Dried Cranberries /Cherries (no sugar added)	¼ cup	123	0	32	2	0	Medium	1.6	1	1.6
Pumpkin Seeds	¼ cup	180	9	8	5	13	-	0	1	0
Total		~695	~20	~52	~13	~49				1.6
Points per Serving									4	0.4

5. Cucumber Bites with Hummus:

These refreshing and flavorful bites are a perfect light snack or appetizer. The cucumber provides hydration and a satisfying crunch, while the hummus offers a creamy and protein-rich dip. It's a simple yet delicious combination that's both nutritious and satisfying.

Prep Time: 5 minutes **Cook Time:** None **Total Time:** 5 minutes **Servings:** Varies (depending on the size of the cucumber and the amount of hummus used)

Ingredients:

- 1 cucumber, sliced
- ½ cup hummus (ensure it is made with zero-point ingredients)

Alternative ingredients for low budget and allergies:

- **Cucumber:** Substitute with bell pepper slices or celery sticks
- **Hummus:** If you don't have hummus or prefer a different flavor, you can substitute it with mashed avocado or another bean dip made with zero-point ingredients

Directions:

1. Wash and slice the cucumber into rounds or sticks
2. Spread or scoop the hummus onto the cucumber slices
3. Enjoy immediately!

Nutritional facts (per serving):

- Will vary depending on the portion size and specific hummus used.
- Refer to the nutritional information of your hummus and adjust accordingly

Special diet specification and recommendation:

- Suitable for vegan and gluten-free diets
- A great option for a quick and healthy snack

Chef tips to make it healthier and faster:

- Prep the cucumber slices ahead of time and store them in an airtight container in the refrigerator for a grab-and-go snack
- Make your own hummus for a fresher and more flavorful dip. You can also experiment with different flavor combinations like roasted red pepper hummus or garlic hummus

Recipe Points: 0 points (assuming hummus is made with zero-point ingredients)

Ingredient	Serving Size	Calories	Protein	Carbs	Fiber	Fat	GI	Points per Serving	Servings Used	Total Points
Cucumber (sliced)	1 medium	45	2	11	2	0	–	0	1	0
Hummus (zero-point)	½ cup	200	8	20	6	10	Low	0	1	0
Total		~245	~10	~31	~8	~10				0
Points per Serving									Varies	0 (assuming moderate portion)

6. Tuna Salad Cucumber Boats

These refreshing cucumber boats offer a light and satisfying snack or light lunch option. The cucumber provides a cool and crisp base, while the tuna salad filling delivers protein and healthy fats. The Greek yogurt adds a touch of creaminess without extra fat, and the fresh dill brings a bright, herbaceous flavor. It's a simple yet delicious way to enjoy a nutritious and satisfying snack.

Prep Time: *10 minutes* **Cook Time:** *None* **Total Time:** *10 minutes* **Servings:** *2*

Ingredients:

- 1 cucumber, halved lengthwise and seeds scooped out
- ½ can tuna in water, drained
- 2 tablespoons plain non-fat Greek yogurt
- 1 tablespoon chopped fresh dill
- Salt and pepper to taste

Alternative Ingredients for Low Budget and Allergies:

- **Tuna:** Substitute with canned salmon or cooked, shredded chicken breast
- **Greek yogurt:** If dairy-free, use a plant-based yogurt alternative.
- **Fresh dill:** Substitute with dried dill or another fresh herb like parsley or chives.

Directions:

1. Cut the cucumber in half lengthwise and use a spoon to scoop out the seeds, creating a boat-like shape
2. In a medium bowl, combine the tuna, Greek yogurt, and dill
3. Season with salt and pepper to taste
4. Fill the cucumber boats with the tuna salad mixture.
5. Enjoy immediately!

Nutritional Facts (per serving):

Macronutrients:
Calories: ~130
Protein: ~15g
Carbs: ~5g
Fiber: ~1g, Fat: ~5g

Micronutrients:
Vitamin D: negligible
Calcium: ~30mg (from yogurt)
Iron: ~1mg
Potassium: ~200mg

Special diet specification and recommendation:

- Suitable for gluten-free and low-carb diets.
- If using dairy-free yogurt, it's also suitable for dairy-free diets

Chef Tips to Make it Healthier and Faster:

- Use a small spoon or melon baller to scoop out the cucumber seeds for a neater presentation
- Add a squeeze of lemon juice to the tuna salad for extra brightness
- If you prefer a spicier tuna salad, add a pinch of red pepper flakes or a dash of hot sauce.

Recipe Points: 0 points (all ingredients are from the no-point food list)

Ingredient	Serving Size	Calories	Protein	Carbs	Fiber	Fat	GI	Points per Serving	Servings Used	Total Points
Cucumber	1 medium	45	2	11	2	0	-	0	1	0
Tuna in water (drained)	½ can (2.5 oz)	60	12.5	0	0	0.5	-	0	1	0
Plain non-fat Greek Yogurt	2 tablespoons	33	5.1	2	0	0	Low	0	1	0
Fresh Dill (chopped)	1 tablespoon	1	0.1	0.2	0.1	0	-	0	1	0
Salt and Pepper	To taste	0	0	0	0	0	-	0	-	0
Total		~139	~19.7	~13.2	~2.1	~0.5				0
Points per Serving									2	0

7. Apple Slices with Almond Butter

This simple and satisfying snack is a perfect combination of sweet and savory flavors. The apple slices provide a refreshing crunch and natural sweetness, while the almond butter offers a dose of protein and healthy fats. It's a quick and easy snack that's both nutritious and delicious, perfect for curbing cravings and keeping you energized.

Prep Time: 5 minutes **Cook Time:** None **Total Time:** 5 minutes **Servings:** 1

Ingredients:

- 1 apple, sliced
- 2 tablespoons almond butter

Alternative Ingredients for Low Budget and Allergies:

- **Apple:** Use any other type of fruit you enjoy, such as pear slices or banana slices
- **Almond Butter:** If you have a nut allergy, substitute with sunflower seed butter or tahini

Directions:

1. Wash and slice the apple
2. Serve the apple slices with almond butter for dipping

Nutritional Facts:

Macronutrients:
Calories: ~295
Protein: ~8g
Carbs: ~33g
Fiber: ~5g
Fat: ~19g

Micronutrients:
Vitamin D: negligible
Calcium: ~30mg
Iron: ~1mg
Potassium: ~350mg

Special diet specification and recommendation:

- Suitable for vegan and gluten-free diets
- A great option for a quick and healthy snack that's packed with nutrients.

Chef tips to make it healthier and faster:

- If you prefer a thinner almond butter for dipping, you can add a small amount of water and stir until smooth.
- Sprinkle a bit of cinnamon on the apple slices for added flavor
- You can also add a sprinkle of chia seeds or flaxseed to the almond butter for extra fiber and omega-3 fatty acids

Recipe Points: 1 point

Ingredient	Serving Size	Calories	Protein	Carbs	Fiber	Fat	GI	Points per Serving	Servings Used	Total Points
Apple (sliced)	1 medium	95	0	25	4	0	Low	0	1	0
Almond Butter	2 tablespoons	190	7	6	3	16	-	1	1	1
Total		~285	~7	~31	~7	~16				1
Points per Serving									1	1

8. Frozen Yogurt Bark

This delightful frozen treat is a healthy and refreshing alternative to ice cream. The Greek yogurt provides a creamy base and a good source of protein, while the mixed berries add natural sweetness and antioxidants. The chopped nuts offer a satisfying crunch and a dose of healthy fats. This simple and delicious snack is perfect for a hot summer day or anytime you're craving something sweet.

Prep Time: 10 minutes **Freeze Time:** 2-3 hours **Total Time:** 2 hours 10 minutes - 2 hours 15 minutes **Servings:** 4

Ingredients:

- 1 cup plain non-fat Greek yogurt
- ½ cup mixed berries
- 1 tablespoon chopped nuts

Alternative ingredients for low budget and allergies:

- **Greek yogurt:** If you don't have Greek yogurt, any plain, non-fat yogurt will work.
- **Berries:** Use any combination of fresh or frozen berries you enjoy
- **Nuts:** Substitute with seeds (pumpkin, sunflower) if you have nut allergies.

Directions:

1. Line a baking sheet with parchment paper
2. Spread the Greek yogurt evenly onto the prepared baking sheet
3. Sprinkle the mixed berries and chopped nuts over the yogurt
4. Freeze for 2-3 hours, or until solid
5. Break the frozen yogurt bark into pieces and enjoy!

Nutritional Facts (per serving):

Macronutrients:
Calories: ~100
Protein: ~8g
Carbs: ~10g
Fiber: ~1g
Fat: ~4g

Micronutrients:

Vitamin D: negligible (unless using fortified yogurt)
Calcium: ~100mg (from yogurt)
Iron: ~1mg , Potassium: ~200mg

Special diet specification and recommendation:

- Suitable for vegetarian diets.
- For a vegan version, use a plant-based yogurt alternative

Chef tips to make it healthier and faster:

- For a fun twist, drizzle the yogurt with a small amount of melted dark chocolate (consider points if applicable) before freezing.
- You can also add a sprinkle of chia seeds or flaxseed for extra fiber and omega-3 fatty acids
- Store the frozen yogurt bark in an airtight container in the freezer for up to a week

Recipe Points: 0 points (all ingredients are from the no-point food list)

Ingredient	Serving Size	Calories	Protein	Carbs	Fiber	Fat	GI	Points per Serving	Servings Used	Total Points
Plain non-fat Greek Yogurt	1 cup	100	17	6	0	0	Low	0	1	0
Mixed Berries	½ cup	31	0.5	7	2	0.25	Low	0	1	0
Chopped Nuts	1 tablespoon	45	1	2	1	4	-	0	1	0
Total		176	18.5	15	3	4.25				0
Points per Serving									4	0

9. Roasted Chickpeas:

These crispy and flavorful roasted chickpeas are a fantastic alternative to unhealthy snacks like chips or crackers. Chickpeas are packed with protein and fiber, keeping you feeling full and satisfied. The combination of paprika and cumin adds a warm and smoky flavor, making this a delicious and nutritious snack that's perfect for any time of day.

Prep Time: *5 minutes* **Cook Time**: *20-25 minutes* **Total Time**: *25-30 minutes* **Servings**: *4*

Ingredients

- 1 can chickpeas, drained and rinsed
- 1 tablespoon olive oil
- ½ teaspoon paprika
- ½ teaspoon cumin
- Salt and pepper to taste

Alternative Ingredients for Low Budget and Allergies:

- You can use dried chickpeas, but they will need to be soaked and cooked before roasting

Directions:

1. Preheat oven to 400°F (200°C).
2. Pat the chickpeas dry with a paper towel to remove excess moisture
3. In a medium bowl, toss the chickpeas with olive oil, paprika, cumin, salt, and pepper until well coated
4. Spread the chickpeas in a single layer on a baking sheet lined with parchment paper.
5. Bake for 20-25 minutes, or until golden brown and crispy, shaking the pan halfway through to ensure even roasting

Nutritional Facts (per serving):

Macronutrients:
Calories: ~150

195

Protein: ~6g, Carbs: ~20g

Fiber: ~5g, Fat: ~6g

Micronutrients:

Vitamin D: negligible

Calcium: ~40mg

Iron: ~2mg

Potassium: ~250mg

Special diet specification and recommendation:

- Suitable for vegan and gluten-free diets
- A great option for a high-protein, high-fiber snack that's perfect for on-the-go

Chef tips to make it healthier and faster:

- For extra crunch, you can air-fry the chickpeas instead of baking them.
- Experiment with different spices and seasonings to create your own unique flavor combinations

Recipe Points: 0.3 points per serving

Ingredient	Serving Size	Calories	Protein	Carbs	Fiber	Fat	GI	Points per Serving	Servings Used	Total Points
Chickpeas (cooked)	1 can (15 oz)	350	20	62	15	3.5	Low	0	1	0
Olive Oil	1 tablespoon	120	0	0	0	14	-	1.2	1	1.2
Paprika & Cumin	-	~0	~0	~0	~0	~0	-	0	-	0
Salt and Pepper	To taste	0	0	0	0	0	-	0	-	0
Total		~470	~20	~62	~15	~17.5				1.2
Points per Serving									4	0.3

10. Hard-Boiled Eggs:

Hard-boiled eggs are a classic and convenient snack that's packed with protein and essential nutrients. They're a great source of choline, which supports brain health, and they also contain lutein and zeaxanthin, antioxidants that promote eye health. Enjoy them as is for a quick and easy snack, or sprinkle with salt and pepper for added flavor

Prep Time: 5 minutes **Cook Time:** 10-12 minutes **Total Time:** 15-17 minutes **Servings:** 2

Ingredients:

- 2 large eggs

Alternative ingredients for low budget and allergies:

- If you have an egg allergy, you can substitute with a handful of nuts or seeds, or a serving of plain non-fat Greek yogurt.

Directions:

1. Place the eggs in a single layer in a saucepan
2. Add enough cold water to cover the eggs by about an inch
3. Bring the water to a rolling boil over medium-high heat
4. Once boiling, turn off the heat, cover the pot with a lid, and let the eggs sit for 10-12 minutes
5. Drain the hot water and immediately run cold water over the eggs to cool them down
6. Peel the eggs and enjoy them as is or sprinkle with salt and pepper to taste

Nutritional Facts (per serving, 1 egg):

Macronutrients:

Calories: ~70
Protein: ~6g
Carbs: ~0g
Fiber: ~0g
Fat: ~5g

Micronutrients:

Vitamin D: ~10% Daily Value
Calcium: ~25mg
Iron: ~1mg

Potassium: ~60mg

Special diet specification and recommendation:

- Suitable for vegetarian and gluten-free diets.
- If you have high cholesterol, limit your intake of egg yolks to no more than 4 per week

Chef tips to make it healthier and faster:

- To make peeling easier, add a teaspoon of baking soda to the water before boiling
- For a flavorful twist, you can add a splash of vinegar or a bay leaf to the boiling water
- Store peeled hard-boiled eggs in an airtight container in the refrigerator for up to a week

Recipe Points: 0.5 points per serving (1 egg)

Ingredient	Serving Size	Calories	Protein	Carbs	Fiber	Fat	GI	Points per Serving	Servings Used	Total Points
Eggs	2 large	140	12	0	0	10	-	1	1	1
Salt and pepper	To taste	0	0	0	0	0	-	0	-	0
Total		140	12	0	0	10				1
Points per Serving									2	0.5

11. Banana "Ice Cream"

This creamy and refreshing treat is a guilt-free way to satisfy your sweet tooth. Made with just one ingredient - frozen bananas - it's a naturally sweet and satisfying dessert that's packed with potassium and fiber. It's a perfect option for a hot summer day or anytime you're craving a healthy and delicious frozen treat.

Prep Time: 5 minutes (plus freezing time for bananas) **Cook Time:** None **Total Time:** 5 minutes (plus freezing time) **Servings:** 1-2

Ingredients

- 2 frozen bananas, sliced

Alternative ingredients for low budget and allergies:

- N/A - This recipe is already budget-friendly and allergy-friendly!

Directions:

1. Peel and slice the bananas.
2. Place the banana slices in a freezer-safe container or bag and freeze for at least 2 hours, or until solid
3. Add the frozen banana slices to a blender or food processor
4. Blend until smooth and creamy, scraping down the sides as needed.
5. Serve immediately and enjoy!

Nutritional Facts (per serving, assuming 2 servings):

Macronutrients:

Calories: ~105
Protein: ~1g
Carbs: ~27g
Fiber: ~3g
Fat: ~0g

Micronutrients:

Vitamin D: negligible
Calcium: ~10mg
Iron: ~0.3mg
Potassium: ~420mg

Special diet specification and recommendation:

- Suitable for vegan and gluten-free diets
- A great option for a low-fat, naturally sweet treat

Chef tips to make it healthier and faster:

- For a creamier texture, you can add a splash of unsweetened almond milk or coconut milk to the blender
- To add more flavor and nutrients, you can blend in other frozen fruits like berries or mango, or add a handful of spinach or kale for a green boost.
- Top with chopped nuts, seeds, or a drizzle of honey (consider points if applicable)

Recipe Points: 0 points (all ingredients are from the no-point food list)

Ingredient	Serving Size	Calories	Protein	Carbs	Fiber	Fat	GI	Points per Serving	Servings Used	Total Points
Banana (frozen, sliced)	2 medium	210	2	54	6	0	Medium	2.7	1	2.7
Total		210	2	54	6	0				2.7
Points per Serving									2	1.35

12. Fruit Salad

This refreshing and colorful fruit salad is a simple yet satisfying snack or light dessert option. It's packed with vitamins, minerals, and antioxidants, and the variety of fruits offers a delightful medley of flavors and textures. The optional addition of chopped mint adds a touch of freshness and herbaceous notes

Prep Time: 10 minutes **Cook Time:** None **Total Time:** 10 minutes **Servings:** 2

Ingredients:

- 1 cup mixed fruits (berries, grapes, melon, chopped apple)
- 1 tablespoon chopped mint (optional)

Alternative Ingredients for Low Budget and Allergies:

- **Fruits:** Use any combination of seasonal fruits that you enjoy
- **Mint:** If you don't have fresh mint, you can omit it or substitute it with another fresh herb like basil

Directions:

1. Wash and prepare all the fruits. Slice or chop them into bite-sized pieces
2. In a medium bowl, combine all the fruits.
3. If desired, add the chopped mint and toss gently to combine
4. Serve immediately or chill in the refrigerator for later.

Nutritional Facts (per serving):

Macronutrients:

Calories: ~80
Protein: ~1g
Carbs: ~20g
Fiber: ~3g
Fat: ~0g

Micronutrients:

Vitamin D: negligible
Calcium: ~20mg
Iron: ~1mg
Potassium: ~300mg

Special diet specification and recommendation:

- Suitable for vegan and gluten-free diets.
- A great option for a light and refreshing snack or dessert

Chef tips to make it healthier and faster:

- Prep the fruit salad ahead of time and store it in an airtight container in the refrigerator for a grab-and-go snack
- Add a squeeze of lime or lemon juice to prevent the fruits from browning.
- If you want to add more protein, consider adding a dollop of plain non-fat Greek yogurt on top.

Recipe Points: 0 points (all ingredients are from the no-point food list)

Ingredient	Serving Size	Calories	Protein	Carbs	Fiber	Fat	GI	Points per Serving	Servings Used	Total Points
Mixed Fruits	1 cup	160	2	40	6	0	Low/Medium	0	1	0
Chopped Mint (optional)	1 tablespoon	~0	~0	~0	~0	~0	-	0	-	0
Total		~160	~2	~40	~6	~0				0
Points per Serving									2	0

13. Avocado Deviled Eggs

These creamy and flavorful deviled eggs are a delightful twist on a classic appetizer or snack. The combination of avocado and Greek yogurt creates a smooth and rich filling, while the lemon juice adds a touch of brightness. They're a satisfying and nutritious option, packed with healthy fats, protein, and essential nutrients.

Prep Time: 15 minutes **Cook Time:** 10-12 minutes (to hard-boil eggs) **Total Time:** 25-27 minutes **Servings:** 6 (12 deviled egg halves)

Ingredients:

- 3 hard-boiled eggs, halved lengthwise
- 1 ripe avocado, mashed
- 1 tablespoon plain non-fat Greek yogurt
- 1 teaspoon lemon juice
- Salt and pepper to taste
- Paprika for garnish

Alternative Ingredients for Low Budget and Allergies:

- **Avocado:** If you have an avocado allergy or it's unavailable, substitute with hummus or mashed chickpeas.
- **Greek Yogurt:** If dairy-free, use a plant-based yogurt alternative

Directions:

1. Carefully remove the yolks from the hard-boiled eggs and place them in a bowl.
2. Mash the yolks with a fork until smooth
3. Add the mashed avocado, Greek yogurt, and lemon juice to the bowl. Mix well until combined
4. Season with salt and pepper to taste
5. Spoon or pipe the filling into the egg white halves
6. Sprinkle with paprika for garnish.
7. Serve immediately or chill in the refrigerator for later

Nutritional Facts (per serving, 2 deviled egg halves):

Macronutrients:
      Calories: ~130
      Protein: ~7g
      Carbs: ~4g
      Fiber: ~1g
      Fat: ~10g

Micronutrients:
      Vitamin D: ~10% Daily Value (from eggs)
      Calcium: ~30mg
      Iron: ~1mg
      Potassium: ~150mg

Special diet specification and recommendation:

- Suitable for gluten-free diets
- If using dairy-free yogurt, it's also suitable for dairy-free diets

Chef tips to make it healthier and faster:

- Hard-boil the eggs in advance to save time
- For a smoother filling, you can blend the yolks, avocado, yogurt, and lemon juice in a food processor
- Add a pinch of cayenne pepper or chopped chives for extra flavor

Recipe Points: 0 points (all ingredients are from the no-point food list)

Ingredient	Serving Size	Calories	Protein	Carbs	Fiber	Fat	GI	Points per Serving	Servings Used	Total Points
Hard-boiled Eggs	3 large	210	18	0	0	15	-	1.5	1	1.5
Avocado (mashed)	1 medium	322	4	17	14	30	Low	0	1	0
Plain non-fat Greek Yogurt	1 tablespoon	16.5	2.5	1	0	0	Low	0	1	0
Lemon Juice	1 teaspoon	1	0	0.3	0	0	-	0	1	0
Salt and Pepper & Paprika	To taste	0	0	0	0	0	-	0	-	0
Total		~549.5	~24.5	~18.3	~14	~45				1.5
Points per Serving									6	0.25

14. Spinach & Feta Mini-Muffins

These savory mini-muffins are a delightful and protein-packed snack or light breakfast option. The spinach adds a boost of vitamins and minerals, while the feta cheese provides a creamy, salty touch. The egg whites act as a binder and contribute additional protein, making these muffins a satisfying and nutritious treat.

Prep Time: *10 minutes* **Cook Time:** *15-20 minutes* **Total Time:** *25-30 minutes* **Servings:** *6*

Ingredients:

- 1 cup chopped spinach
- ½ cup crumbled feta cheese
- 6 egg whites
- Salt and pepper to taste

Alternative Ingredients for Low Budget and Allergies:

- **Spinach:** Substitute with any other leafy green like kale or Swiss chard, finely chopped
- **Feta Cheese:** If you're watching your points or have dietary restrictions, you can omit the feta cheese or use a smaller amount.

Directions:

1. Preheat oven to 350°F (175°C). Grease a muffin tin.
2. In a medium bowl, whisk the egg whites until frothy
3. Season the egg whites with salt and pepper to taste
4. Gently stir in the chopped spinach and crumbled feta cheese
5. Divide the mixture evenly among the greased muffin tins
6. Bake for 15-20 minutes, or until the muffins are set and lightly golden on top

Nutritional Facts (per serving, 1 muffin):

Macronutrients:

Calories: ~60
Protein: ~8g
Carbs: ~2g
Fiber: ~1g
Fat: ~3g

Micronutrients: Vitamin D: negligible

Calcium: ~80mg

Iron: ~1mg, Potassium: ~100mg

Special diet specification and recommendation:

- Suitable for vegetarian and gluten-free diets
- A great option for a high-protein, low-carb snack or breakfast

Chef tips to make it healthier and faster:

- You can use pre-washed and chopped spinach to save on prep time
- Add a pinch of red pepper flakes or other herbs and spices for extra flavor
- Store leftover muffins in an airtight container in the refrigerator for up to 3 days

Recipe Points: 0 points (all ingredients are from the no-point food list)

Ingredient	Serving Size	Calories	Protein	Carbs	Fiber	Fat	GI	Points per Serving	Servings Used	Total Points
Spinach (cooked)	1 cup	41	5	7	4	0.4	Low	0	1	0
Feta Cheese (crumbled)	½ cup	200	12	8	0	16	-	2	1	2
Egg whites	6	102	24	0	0	0	-	0	1	0
Salt and Pepper	To taste	0	0	0	0	0	-	0	-	0
Total		~343	~41	~15	~4	~16.4				2
Points per Serving									6	0.33

15. Spiced Fruit & Nut Parfait

This delightful parfait is a perfect healthy and satisfying snack or light dessert. The creamy Greek yogurt provides a good source of protein, while the mixed fruits offer natural sweetness, vitamins, and antioxidants. The chopped walnuts add a satisfying crunch and a dose of healthy fats. The sprinkle of cinnamon and nutmeg adds warmth and spice, making this a comforting and flavorful treat.

Prep Time: 5 minutes **Cook Time:** None **Total Time:** 5 minutes **Servings:** 1

Ingredients:

- ½ cup plain non-fat Greek yogurt
- ½ cup chopped mixed fruits (apple, pear, grapes)
- ¼ cup chopped walnuts
- Sprinkle of cinnamon & nutmeg

Alternative ingredients for low budget and allergies:

- **Greek Yogurt:** If you don't have Greek yogurt, any plain non-fat yogurt will work.
- **Mixed Fruits:** Use any combination of fruits you enjoy
- **Walnuts:** Substitute with other nuts or seeds if you have nut allergies

Directions:

1. In a glass or bowl, layer the Greek yogurt, chopped mixed fruits, and chopped walnuts
2. Repeat the layers as desired, ending with a layer of yogurt
3. Sprinkle with cinnamon and nutmeg
4. Enjoy immediately!

Nutritional Facts:

Macronutrients:

Calories: ~300
Protein: ~10g
Carbs: ~30g
Fiber: ~5g
Fat: ~18g

Micronutrients:

     Vitamin D: negligible (unless using fortified yogurt)
     Calcium: ~100mg (from yogurt)
     Iron: ~1.5mg
     Potassium: ~350mg

Special diet specification and recommendation:

- Suitable for vegetarian diets
- For a vegan option, use a plant-based yogurt alternative

Chef tips to make it healthier and faster:

- Prep individual servings in jars or containers ahead of time for a grab-and-go snack
- If you prefer a sweeter parfait, drizzle with a small amount of honey or maple syrup (consider points if applicable)

Recipe Points: 0 points (all ingredients are from the no-point food list)

Ingredient	Serving Size	Calories	Protein	Carbs	Fiber	Fat	GI	Points per Serving	Servings Used	Total Points
Plain non-fat Greek Yogurt	½ cup	50	8.5	3	0	0	Low	0	1	0
Mixed Fruits (chopped)	½ cup	80	1	20	3	0	Low/Medium	0	1	0
Walnuts (chopped)	¼ cup	185	4	4	2	18	-	0	1	0
Cinnamon & Nutmeg	Sprinkle	~0	~0	~0	~0	~0	-	0	-	0
Total		~315	~13.5	~27	~5	~18				0
Points per Serving									1	0

Special Occasion Recipes

1. Grilled Salmon with Lemon-Dill Yogurt Sauce & Asparagus

This elegant dish is perfect for a special occasion, showcasing the delicate flavors of grilled salmon paired with a refreshing lemon-dill yogurt sauce and vibrant asparagus. The salmon, rich in omega-3 fatty acids, is a heart-healthy protein source. The asparagus adds a touch of springtime freshness and provides essential nutrients. The yogurt sauce, infused with zesty lemon and fragrant dill, adds a creamy and flavorful element that complements the grilled salmon and asparagus beautifully.

Prep Time: 15 minutes **Cook Time:** 12-15 minutes **Total Time:** 27-30 minutes **Servings:** 4**Ingredients:**

- 4 salmon fillets
- 1 lemon, zested and juiced
- 1 tablespoon olive oil
- Salt and pepper to taste
- 1 bunch asparagus, trimmed
- ½ cup plain non-fat Greek yogurt
- 1 tablespoon chopped fresh dill

Alternative ingredients for low budget and allergies:

- **Salmon:** Substitute with another type of fish like cod or tilapia.
- **Asparagus:** If asparagus is unavailable or not preferred, substitute with another green vegetable like broccoli florets or green beans.

Directions:

1. Preheat your grill to medium-high heat
2. Season the salmon fillets with salt, pepper, lemon zest, and juice. Drizzle with olive oil
3. Toss the asparagus with a drizzle of olive oil, salt, and pepper
4. Grill the salmon for 5-7 minutes per side, or until cooked through
5. Grill t
6. he asparagus for 3-5 minutes, or until tender-crisp
7. While the salmon and asparagus are grilling, combine the Greek yogurt and chopped fresh dill in a small bowl to make the sauce
8. Serve the grilled salmon with the asparagus and a dollop of the lemon-dill yogurt sauce

Nutritional facts (per serving):

Macronutrients:

Calories: ~350
Protein: ~35g
Carbs: ~10g
Fiber: ~3g
Fat: ~18g

Micronutrients:

Vitamin D: ~60% Daily Value (from salmon)
Calcium: ~100mg (from yogurt)
Iron: ~2mg
Potassium: ~700mg

Special diet specification and recommendation:

- Suitable for gluten-free and dairy-free diets (if using dairy-free yogurt)
- A great option for a special occasion meal that's both healthy and delicious

Chef tips to make it healthier and cook faster:

- To ensure even cooking, choose salmon fillets that are similar in size and thickness
- If you don't have a grill, you can bake the salmon and asparagus in a preheated oven at 400F for about 12-15 minutes.

Recipe Points: 0 points (all ingredients are from the no-point food list)

Ingredient	Serving Size	Calories	Protein	Carbs	Fiber	Fat	GI	Points per Serving	Servings Used	Total Points
Salmon Fillets	4 (4 oz each)	680	88	0	0	40	Low	0	1	0
Asparagus	1 bunch	100	8	18	8	0.5	Low	0	1	0
Plain non-fat Greek Yogurt	½ cup	50	8.5	3	0	0	Low	0	1	0
Fresh Dill (chopped)	1 tablespoon	1	0.1	0.2	0.1	0	-	0	1	0
Olive Oil	1 tablespoon	120	0	0	0	14	-	1.2	1	1.2
Lemon (zest and juice)	1 medium	20	0.5	5	1.5	0	-	0	1	0
Salt and Pepper	To taste	0	0	0	0	0	-	0	-	0
Total		~971	~105.1	~26.2	~11.1	~54.5				1.2
Points per Serving									4	0.3

2. Mediterranean Stuffed Chicken Breast

This dish elevates the humble chicken breast into a special occasion meal. The stuffing, a medley of feta cheese, spinach, and Kalamata olives, adds a burst of Mediterranean flavors and textures. Baking the chicken ensures it stays moist and tender, while the stuffing creates a delightful surprise in every bite.

Prep Time: 15 minutes **Cook Time**: 20-25 minutes **Total Time**: 35-40 minutes **Servings**: 4

Ingredients

- 4 boneless, skinless chicken breasts
- ½ cup crumbled feta cheese
- ½ cup chopped spinach
- ¼ cup chopped Kalamata olives
- 1 tablespoon chopped fresh oregano
- Salt and pepper to taste

Alternative Ingredients for Low Budget and Allergies:

- **Feta Cheese:** Substitute with crumbled goat cheese or ricotta cheese (consider points if using full-fat versions)
- **Spinach:** If you don't have fresh spinach, you can use frozen spinach, thawed and squeezed dry

Directions

1. Preheat oven to 375F
2. Using a sharp knife, butterfly each chicken breast, creating a pocket
3. In a medium bowl, combine feta cheese, spinach, olives, and oregano
4. Stuff each chicken breast with the filling mixture
5. Season the chicken breasts with salt and pepper
6. Place the stuffed chicken breasts in a baking dish and bake for 20-25 minutes, or until cooked through (internal temperature reaches 165°F)

Nutritional Facts (per serving):

Macronutrients:

Calories: ~300

Protein: ~40g

Carbs: ~5g

Fiber: ~2g

Fat: ~15g

Micronutrients:

Vitamin D: negligible

Calcium: ~150mg

Iron: ~2mg

Potassium: ~400mg

Special diet specification and recommendation:

- Suitable for gluten-free diets

Chef tips to make it healthier and faster:

- You can pound the chicken breasts slightly to ensure even thickness and faster cooking
- If you don't have fresh oregano, you can use dried oregano, but reduce the amount by half.
- Serve with a side of roasted vegetables or a salad for a complete meal.

Ingredient	Serving Size	Calories	Protein	Carbs	Fiber	Fat	GI	Points per Serving	Servings Used	Total Points
Chicken Breasts (boneless, skinless)	4 (3 oz each)	560	104	0	0	12	–	0	1	0
Feta Cheese (crumbled)	½ cup	200	12	8	0	16	–	2	1	2
Spinach (cooked)	½ cup	20.5	2.5	3.5	2	0.2	Low	0	1	0
Kalamata Olives (chopped)	¼ cup	50	0	1	1	5	–	0	1	0
Fresh Oregano (chopped)	1 tablespoon	3	0.3	0.6	0.3	0.1	–	0	1	0
Salt and Pepper	To taste	0	0	0	0	0	–	0	–	0
Total		~833.5	~120.3	~13.1	~3.3	~33.3				2
Points per Serving									4	0.5

216

3. Roasted Vegetable Tart

This vibrant and flavorful tart is a delightful vegetarian option that's perfect for a special occasion or a shared meal. The colorful array of roasted vegetables provides essential vitamins, minerals, and antioxidants, while the whole-wheat pie crust offers a hearty and satisfying base. The crumbled feta cheese adds a touch of creamy saltiness, and the simple seasoning of olive oil and thyme enhances the natural flavors of the vegetables.

Prep Time: 20 minutes **Cook Time:** 25-30 minutes **Total Time:** 45-50 minutes **Servings:** 6

Ingredients:

- 1 pre-made whole wheat pie crust (ensure it's made with zero-point ingredients)
- 1 cup sliced zucchini
- 1 cup sliced eggplant
- 1 cup sliced bell peppers (any color)
- 1 cup cherry tomatoes, halved
- 1 red onion, sliced
- 2 tablespoons olive oil
- ½ teaspoon dried thyme
- Salt and pepper to taste
- ¼ cup crumbled feta cheese

Alternative Ingredients for Low Budget and Allergies:

- **Pre-made pie crust:** If you prefer, you can make your own whole-wheat pie crust using whole-wheat flour, olive oil, and water.
- **Vegetables:** Feel free to use any combination of your favorite vegetables, such as mushrooms, asparagus, or butternut squash.
- **Feta Cheese:** If you're watching your points or have dietary restrictions, you can omit the feta cheese or use a smaller amount.

Directions:

1. Preheat your oven to 400°F (200°C).
2. In a large bowl, toss the sliced zucchini, eggplant, bell peppers, cherry tomatoes, and red onion with the olive oil, dried thyme, salt, and pepper until well coated
3. Arrange the vegetables in the pre-made whole-wheat pie crust

4. Sprinkle the crumbled feta cheese evenly over the vegetables.
5. Bake in the preheated oven for 25-30 minutes, or until the vegetables are tender and the crust is golden brown

Nutritional facts (per serving):

Macronutrients:

Calories: ~250

Protein: ~7g

Carbs: ~30g

Fiber: ~5g

Fat: ~13g

Micronutrients:

Vitamin D: negligible

Calcium: ~100mg (from feta cheese)

Iron: ~2mg

Potassium: ~400mg

Special diet specification and recommendation:

- Can be easily adapted for vegan diets by omitting the feta cheese or using a vegan cheese alternative
- A great option for a colorful and flavorful vegetarian meal that is perfect for sharing

Chef tips to make it healthier and faster:

- You can roast the vegetables ahead of time to save on prep time
- If you prefer a crispier crust, you can pre-bake the pie crust for a few minutes before adding the vegetables
- Serve with a side salad or a dollop of plain yogurt for a complete meal (consider points if applicable)

Recipe Points: 1.2 points per serving

Ingredient	Serving Size	Calories	Protein	Carbs	Fiber	Fat	GI	Points per Serving	Servings Used	Total Points
Whole Wheat Pie Crust (zero-point)	1	~200	~5	~30	~4	~8	Medium	1.5	1	1.5
Zucchini (sliced)	1 cup	19	1	4	1	0.4	Low	0	1	0
Eggplant (sliced)	1 cup	20	1	5	2	0	Low	0	1	0
Bell Peppers (sliced)	1 cup	45	1.5	10	3	0	Low	0	1	0
Cherry Tomatoes (halved)	1 cup	25	1	6	1.5	0	Low	0	1	0
Red Onion (sliced)	1 medium	64	1.5	15	2	0	-	0	1	0
Olive Oil	2 tablespoons	240	0	0	0	28	-	2.8	1	2.8
Dried Thyme	½ teaspoon	2	0.1	0.4	0.2	0.1	-	0	1	0
Salt and Pepper	To taste	0	0	0	0	0	-	0	-	0

Feta Cheese (crumbled)	¼ cup	100	6	4	0	8	–	1	1	1
Total		~815	~16.6	~74.4	~13.7	~44.5				5.3
Points per Serving									6	0.88

4. Shrimp & Vegetable Skewers with Lemon-Garlic Marinade

These vibrant skewers are a delightful and healthy option, perfect for a light dinner or a special occasion appetizer. The colorful vegetables, grilled to perfection, offer a variety of textures and nutrients. The succulent shrimp, marinated in a zesty lemon-garlic mixture, adds a burst of flavor and lean protein.

Prep Time: 20 minutes **Cook Time:** 10-12 minutes **Total Time:** 30-32 minutes **Servings:** 4**Ingredients:**

- 1 pound large shrimp, peeled and deveined
- 1 zucchini, cut into chunks
- 1 bell pepper, cut into chunks
- 1 red onion, cut into chunks
- 1 lemon, zested and juiced
- 2 cloves garlic, minced
- 2 tablespoons olive oil
- Salt and pepper to taste

Alternative Ingredients for Low Budget and Allergies:

- **Shrimp:** Substitute with firm tofu cubes or tempeh cubes, marinated in the same way
- **Vegetables:** Feel free to use any combination of your favorite vegetables, such as mushrooms, eggplant, or yellow squash

Directions:

1. In a small bowl, combine lemon zest, lemon juice, garlic, olive oil, salt, and pepper for the marinade
2. Thread shrimp, zucchini, bell pepper, and onion onto skewers
3. Marinate skewers for 30 minutes
4. Grill skewers over medium heat for 5-7 minutes per side, or until shrimp is cooked through and vegetables are tender

Macronutrients:

      Calories: ~250

      Protein: ~28g

      Carbs: ~12g

      Fiber: ~3g

      Fat: ~10g

Micronutrients:

      Vitamin D: negligible

      Calcium: ~60mg

      Iron: ~3mg

      Potassium: ~450mg

Special diet specification and recommendation:

- Suitable for gluten-free diets
- Can be easily adapted for vegetarian or vegan diets by substituting the shrimp with tofu or tempeh

Chef tips to make it healthier and faster:

- Soak the skewers in water for 30 minutes before assembling to prevent them from burning on the grill
- Marinate the shrimp and vegetables for at least 30 minutes, or up to overnight, for maximum flavor
- Serve with a side of brown rice or quinoa (consider points if applicable) and a dollop of tzatziki for a complete meal

Recipe Points: 0.3 points per serving

Ingredient	Serving Size	Calories	Protein	Carbs	Fiber	Fat	GI	Points per Serving	Servings Used	Total Points
Shrimp (peeled & deveined)	1 pound	500	100	0	0	10	–	0	1	0
Zucchini (chunks)	1 medium	33	2	6	2	0.4	Low	0	1	0
Bell Pepper (chunks)	1 medium	30	1	7	2	0	Low	0	1	0
Red Onion (chunks)	1 medium	6								

5. Mediterranean Lentil Loaf

This hearty and flavorful lentil loaf is a vegetarian delight, packed with protein and fiber from the lentils. The combination of vegetables and herbs creates a savory and satisfying loaf that's perfect for a special occasion or a comforting weeknight meal. Baking the loaf ensures a firm and golden brown crust, while the interior remains moist and tender.

Prep Time: *20 minutes* **Cook Time**: *30-35 minutes* **Total Time**: *50-55 minutes* **Servings**: 6

Ingredients:

- 2 cups cooked lentils
- 1 cup chopped onion
- 1 cup chopped carrots
- 1 cup chopped mushrooms
- 2 cloves garlic, minced
- 1 egg
- ½ cup whole wheat breadcrumbs
- ½ teaspoon dried oregano
- ½ teaspoon dried thyme
- Salt and pepper to taste

Alternative Ingredients for Low Budget and Allergies:

- **Lentils:** Substitute with another type of cooked legume, such as black beans or chickpeas.
- **Egg:** For a vegan option, use a flax egg (1 tablespoon ground flaxseed mixed with 3 tablespoons water) or mashed sweet potato as a binder.
- **Whole Wheat Breadcrumbs:** Substitute with almond flour or oat flour for a gluten-free option.

Directions:

1. Preheat oven to 375°F (190°C)
2. Heat a drizzle of olive oil in a large skillet over medium heat
3. Add the chopped onion, carrots, and mushrooms, and sauté until softened, about 5-7 minutes.

4. Add the minced garlic, dried oregano, and thyme. Cook for 1 minute more, stirring frequently
5. In a large bowl, combine the cooked lentils, sautéed vegetables, egg, breadcrumbs, salt, and pepper. Mix well until all the ingredients are combined
6. Transfer the mixture to a greased loaf pan
7. Bake in the preheated oven for 30-35 minutes, or until the loaf is firm and golden brown on top.
8. Let the loaf cool slightly before slicing and serving.

Nutritional Facts (per serving):

Macronutrients:

Calories: ~250
Protein: ~15g
Carbs: ~35g
Fiber: ~8g
Fat: ~5g

Micronutrients:

Vitamin D: negligible
Calcium: ~40mg
Iron: ~4mg
Potassium: ~500mg

Special diet specification and recommendation:

- Can be easily adapted for vegan and gluten-free diets (with substitutions mentioned above)
- A great option for a hearty and satisfying vegetarian meal.

Chef tips to make it healthier and faster:

- Use pre-cooked lentils to save time
- If the mixture is too wet, add a bit more breadcrumbs to help it hold its shape
- Serve with a side salad or roasted vegetables for a complete meal.

Ingredient	Serving Size	Calories	Protein	Carbs	Fiber	Fat	GI	Points per Serving	Servings Used	Total Points
Lentils (cooked)	2 cups	460	36	80	32	2	Low	0	1	0
Onion (chopped)	1 medium	64	1.5	15	2	0	-	0	1	0
Carrots (chopped)	1 cup	51	1.1	12	3.4	0.2	Low	0	1	0
Mushrooms (chopped)	1 cup	17	2.3	3	2	0.3	-	0	1	0
Garlic (minced)	2 cloves	9	0.5	2	0.2	0	-	0	1	0
Egg	1 large	70	6	0	0	5	-	0.5	1	0.5
Whole Wheat Breadcrumbs	½ cup	160	6	28	3	1	Medium	1.5	1	1.5
Dried Oregano & Thyme	-	~0	~0	~0	~0	~0	-	0	-	0
Salt and Pepper	To taste	0	0	0	0	0	-	0	-	0
Total		~931	~53.4	~140	~42.6	~8.5				2
Points per Serving									6	0.33

6. Baked Cod with Mediterranean Crust

This elegant dish features flaky cod fillets coated in a flavorful Mediterranean crust, creating a delightful combination of textures and tastes. The lemon zest and juice add brightness, while the garlic and parsley infuse the fish with aromatic notes. The whole-wheat breadcrumbs and Parmesan cheese create a crispy and golden crust, making this a special occasion meal that's both healthy and delicious.

Prep Time: *15 minutes* ***Cook Time***: *15-20 minutes* ***Total Time***: *30-35 minutes* ***Servings***: *4*

Ingredients:

- 4 cod fillets
- ½ cup whole wheat breadcrumbs
- ¼ cup chopped fresh parsley
- ¼ cup grated Parmesan cheese (consider points if using full-fat)
- 1 tablespoon olive oil
- 1 lemon, zested
- Salt and pepper to taste

Alternative Ingredients for Low Budget and Allergies:

- **Cod:** Substitute with another type of white fish, such as tilapia or haddock
- **Parmesan Cheese:** If you're watching your points or have dietary restrictions, you can omit the Parmesan cheese or use a smaller amount

Directions:

1. Preheat oven to 400F
2. In a small bowl, combine breadcrumbs, parsley, Parmesan cheese, olive oil and lemon zest
3. Season cod fillets with salt and pepper
4. Press breadcrumb mixture onto the top of each fillet
5. Bake for 15-20 minutes or until cod is cooked through and crust is golden brown

Nutritional facts (per serving):

Macronutrients:

      Calories: ~280

      Protein: ~30g

      Carbs: ~20g

      Fiber: ~3g

      Fat: ~12g

Micronutrients:

      Vitamin D: ~10% Daily Value

      Calcium: ~150mg (from Parmesan cheese)

      Iron: ~1mg

      Potassium: ~400mg

Special diet specification and recommendation

- Easily adaptable for gluten-free diets (use gluten-free breadcrumbs)
- A great option for a special occasion meal that's both healthy and delicious

Chef tips to make it healthier and cook faster:

- If you don't have fresh parsley, you can use dried parsley, but reduce the amount by half
- Serve with a side of steamed or roasted vegetables for a complete meal.

Ingredient	Serving Size	Calories	Protein	Carbs	Fiber	Fat	GI	Points per Serving	Servings Used	Total Points
Cod Fillets	4 (4 oz each)	320	64	0	0	8	–	0	1	0
Whole Wheat Breadcrumbs	½ cup	160	6	28	3	1	Medium	1.5	1	1.5
Fresh Parsley (chopped)	¼ cup	2	0.2	0.4	0.2	0	–	0	1	0
Parmesan Cheese (grated)	¼ cup	110	14	1	0	7	–	1	1	1
Olive Oil	1 tablespoon	120	0	0	0	14	–	1.2	1	1.2
Lemon (zest)	1 medium	5	0.1	1	0.3	0	–	0	1	0

7. Grilled Portobello Mushroom Steaks with Balsamic Glaze

These hearty and flavorful portobello mushroom steaks are a fantastic vegetarian option that's perfect for a special occasion or a satisfying meatless Monday meal. The mushrooms, marinated in a simple balsamic glaze, are grilled to perfection, creating a tender and juicy texture with a slightly sweet and tangy flavor. It's a delicious and nutritious dish that's sure to impress even the most discerning palates.

Prep Time: *15 minutes* **Cook Time**: *10-12 minutes* **Total Time**: *25-27 minutes* **Servings**: 4

Ingredients

- 4 large portobello mushrooms, stems removed
- 2 tablespoons balsamic vinegar
- 1 tablespoon olive oil
- 1 clove garlic, minced
- Salt and pepper to taste

Alternative Ingredients for Low Budget and Allergies:

- **Portobello Mushrooms**: If portobello mushrooms are unavailable or not preferred, you can substitute them with large white button mushrooms or cremini mushrooms.

Directions:

1. In a small bowl, whisk together the balsamic vinegar, olive oil, minced garlic, salt, and pepper to make the marinade.
2. Brush the portobello mushrooms generously with the marinade, ensuring both sides are well coated
3. Preheat the grill to medium-high heat
4. Place the marinated mushrooms on the grill and cook for 5-7 minutes per side, or until tender and slightly charred

Macronutrients:

      Calories: ~100

      Protein: ~3g

      Carbs: ~10g

      Fiber: ~2g

      Fat: ~6g

Micronutrients:

      Vitamin D: negligible

      Calcium: ~20mg

      Iron: ~1mg

      Potassium: ~300mg

Special diet specification and recommendation:

- Suitable for vegan and gluten-free diets
- A great option for a hearty and flavorful vegetarian meal that is also low in calories

Chef tips to make it healthier and faster:

- If you don't have a grill, you can broil the mushrooms in the oven for a similar effect
- For a more intense flavor, you can marinate the mushrooms for longer, even up to overnight in the refrigerator
- Serve the grilled mushrooms on a bed of mixed greens or with a side of roasted vegetables for a complete meal.

Ingredient	Serving Size	Calories	Protein	Carbs	Fiber	Fat	GI	Points per Serving	Servings Used	Total Points
Portobello Mushrooms	4 large	120	12	20	8	0	-	0	1	0
Balsamic Vinegar	2 tablespoons	28	0	6	0	0	-	0	1	0
Olive Oil	1 tablespoon	120	0	0	0	14	-	1.2	1	1.2
Garlic (minced)	1 clove	4.5	0.2	1	0.1	0	-	0	1	0
Salt and Pepper	To taste	0	0	0	0	0	-	0	-	0
Total		~272.5	~12.2	~27	~8.1	~14				1.2
Points per Serving									4	0.3

232

8. Mediterranean Quinoa Salad with Shrimp

This vibrant and refreshing salad is a delightful combination of textures and flavors, perfect for a light lunch or dinner. The quinoa provides a hearty base of protein and fiber, while the shrimp adds lean protein and a touch of sweetness. The colorful vegetables and olives bring a burst of freshness and antioxidants, and the feta cheese adds a creamy, salty element. The lemon vinaigrette ties everything together with a zesty and flavorful touch.

Prep Time: 15 minutes **Cook Time:** 10-12 minutes (for cooking quinoa) **Total Time:** 25-27 minutes **Servings:** 4

Ingredients:

- 1 cup cooked quinoa
- ½ pound cooked shrimp, peeled and deveined
- 1 cup chopped cucumber
- 1 cup cherry tomatoes, halved
- ½ cup Kalamata olives, pitted and halved
- ¼ cup chopped red onion
- ¼ cup crumbled feta cheese
- 2 tablespoons chopped fresh dill
- Lemon vinaigrette (made with olive oil, lemon juice, Dijon mustard, garlic, salt, and pepper)

Alternative ingredients for low budget and allergies:

- **Shrimp:** Substitute with canned tuna or salmon, or another cooked protein source like chickpeas or lentils.
- **Feta Cheese:** If you're watching your points or have dietary restrictions, you can omit the feta cheese or use a smaller amount.

Directions:

1. If you're not using pre-cooked quinoa, cook it according to package directions
2. In a large bowl, combine the cooked quinoa, cooked shrimp, chopped cucumber, halved cherry tomatoes, Kalamata olives, red onion, crumbled feta cheese, and chopped dill.
3. In a small bowl, whisk together the olive oil, lemon juice, Dijon mustard, minced garlic, salt, and pepper to make the vinaigrette

4. Pour the vinaigrette over the salad and toss to coat evenly
5. Serve chilled or at room temperature

Macronutrients:

Calories: ~300

Protein: ~20g

Carbs: ~25g

Fiber: ~5g

Fat: ~13g

Micronutrients:

Vitamin D: negligible

Calcium: ~80mg

Iron: ~2mg

Potassium: ~450mg

Special diet specification and recommendation:

- Suitable for gluten-free diets.
- A great option for a light and refreshing mcal that's packed with protein and healthy fats.

Chef tips to make it healthier and faster:

- Cook the quinoa and shrimp ahead of time and store them in the refrigerator for quick assembly.
- Make a large batch of lemon vinaigrette to have on hand for future salads.
- Add a handful of chopped nuts or seeds for extra crunch and healthy fats

Recipe Points: 0.8 points per serving

Ingredient	Serving Size	Calories	Protein	Carbs	Fiber	Fat	GI	Points per Serving	Servings Used	Total Points
Quinoa (cooked)	1 cup	222	8	40	5	4	Low	0	1	0
Shrimp (cooked)	½ pound	250	50	0	0	5	-	0	1	0
Cucumber (chopped)	1 cup	16	1	4	1	0	-	0	1	0
Cherry Tomatoes (halved)	1 cup	25	1	6	1.5	0	Low	0	1	0
Kalamata Olives (pitted & halved)	½ cup	100	0	2	2	10	-	0	1	0
Red Onion (chopped)	¼ cup	16	0.4	4	0.6	0	-	0	1	0
Feta Cheese (crumbled)	¼ cup	100	6	4	0	8	-	1	1	1
Fresh Dill (chopped)	2 tablespoons	2	0.2	0.4	0.2	0	-	0	1	0

Lemon Vinaigrette	(let's assume 2 tbsp total)	120	0	3	0	13	–	1.3	1	1.3
Salt and Pepper	To taste	0	0	0	0	0	–	0	–	0
Total		~1251	~67	~63.4	~10.3	~39				2.3
Points per Serving									4	0.575

9. Spinach and Feta Stuffed Salmon

This elegant and flavorful dish is a perfect centerpiece for a special occasion. The flaky salmon fillets are stuffed with a vibrant mixture of spinach, feta cheese, and dill, creating a delightful combination of textures and tastes. Baking the salmon ensures it stays moist and tender, while the stuffing adds a burst of Mediterranean flavors.

Prep Time: 15 minutes **Cook Time:** 15-20 minutes **Total Time:** 30-35 minutes **Servings:** 4

Ingredients:

- 4 salmon fillets
- 1 cup chopped spinach
- ½ cup crumbled feta cheese
- ¼ cup chopped fresh dill
- 1 tablespoon olive oil
- Salt and pepper to taste

Alternative Ingredients for Low Budget and Allergies:

- **Salmon:** Substitute with another type of fish like cod or tilapia
- **Feta Cheese:** Substitute with crumbled goat cheese or ricotta cheese (consider points if using full-fat versions)
- **Spinach:** If you don't have fresh spinach, you can use frozen spinach, thawed and squeezed dry

Directions:

1. Preheat the oven to 400F.
2. Using a sharp knife, make a slit in the side of each salmon fillet to create a pocket.
3. In a medium bowl, combine the chopped spinach, crumbled feta cheese, and chopped fresh dill.
4. Stuff each salmon fillet with the filling mixture
5. Drizzle the salmon fillets with olive oil and season with salt and pepper to taste
6. Place the stuffed salmon fillets on a baking sheet lined with parchment paper
7. Bake in the preheated oven for 15-20 minutes, or until the salmon is cooked through and flakes easily with a fork

Nutritional Facts (per serving):

- **Macronutrients:**
  - Calories: ~350
  - Protein: ~35g
  - Carbs: ~5g
  - Fiber: ~2g
  - Fat: ~20g
- **Micronutrients:**
  - Vitamin D: ~50% Daily Value (from salmon)
  - Calcium: ~100mg (from feta cheese)
  - Iron: ~2mg
  - Potassium: ~500mg

Special diet specification and recommendation:

- Suitable for gluten-free diets
- A great option for a special occasion meal that's both healthy and delicious.

Chef tips to make it healthier and cook faster:

- You can use pre-washed and chopped spinach to save on prep time.
- Add a squeeze of lemon juice to the filling for extra brightness
- Serve with a side of steamed or roasted vegetables for a complete meal.

Recipe Points: 0.7 points per serving

Ingredient	Serving Size	Calories	Protein	Carbs	Fiber	Fat	GI	Points per Serving	Servings Used	Total Points
Salmon Fillets	4 (4 oz each)	680	88	0	0	40	-	0	1	0
Spinach (cooked)	1 cup	41	5	7	4	0.4	Low	0	1	0
Feta Cheese (crumbled)	½ cup	200	12	8	0	16	-	2	1	2
Fresh Dill (chopped)	¼ cup	2.5	0.25	0.5	0.25	0	-	0	1	0
Olive Oil	1 tablespoon	120	0	0	0	14	-	1.2	1	1.2
Salt and pepper	To taste	0	0	0	0	0	-	0	-	0
Total		~1043.5	~105.25	~15.5	~4.25	~70.4				3.2
Points per Serving									4	0.8

239

10. Mediterranean Vegetable Curry

This aromatic and flavorful curry is a celebration of Mediterranean vegetables and spices, offering a vibrant and satisfying vegetarian meal. The combination of eggplant, zucchini, and cauliflower creates a medley of textures, while the blend of curry powder, cumin, coriander, and turmeric infuses the dish with warmth and depth. Served over brown rice, this curry is a nutritious and delicious option that's perfect for a special occasion or a comforting weeknight dinner.

Prep Time: 20 minutes **Cook Time:** 25-30 minutes **Total Time:** 45-50 minutes **Servings:** 4

Ingredients:

- 1 tablespoon olive oil
- 1 onion, chopped
- 2 cloves garlic, minced
- 1 teaspoon curry powder
- ½ teaspoon ground cumin
- ½ teaspoon ground coriander
- ½ teaspoon turmeric
- 1 can (14.5 oz) diced tomatoes
- 1 cup vegetable broth
- 1 cup chopped eggplant
- 1 cup chopped zucchini
- 1 cup cauliflower florets
- Salt and pepper to taste
- Chopped fresh cilantro for garnish
- Cooked brown rice for serving

Alternative Ingredients for Low Budget and Allergies:

- **Vegetables:** Feel free to substitute or add any other vegetables you enjoy, such as bell peppers, potatoes, or green beans.
- **Spices:** If you prefer a milder curry, you can reduce the amount of curry powder or omit some of the spices.

Directions:

1. Heat the olive oil in a large pot or Dutch oven over medium heat.
2. Add the chopped onion and cook until softened, about 5 minutes.
3. Add the minced garlic, curry powder, cumin, coriander, and turmeric. Cook for 1 minute more, stirring constantly.
4. Stir in the diced tomatoes, vegetable broth, eggplant, zucchini, and cauliflower florets.
5. Season with salt and pepper to taste.
6. Bring the mixture to a boil, then reduce heat to low, cover, and simmer for 15-20 minutes, or until the vegetables are tender.
7. Garnish with chopped fresh cilantro and serve over cooked brown rice.

Nutritional Facts (per serving):

Macronutrients:

Calories: ~300 (without brown rice)
Protein: ~5g
Carbs: ~40g
Fiber: ~7g
Fat: ~12g

Micronutrients:

Vitamin D: negligible
Calcium: ~50mg
Iron: ~2mg
Potassium: ~600mg

Special diet specification and recommendation:

- Suitable for vegan and gluten-free diets
- A great option for a flavorful and satisfying vegetarian meal.

Chef tips to make it healthier and cook faster:

- Use pre-chopped vegetables to save on prep time
- If you prefer a thicker curry, you can add a tablespoon of cornstarch mixed with 2 tablespoons of water to the pot during the last few minutes of cooking.
- Serve with a dollop of plain yogurt for extra creaminess and protein (consider points if applicable).

Recipe Points: 1.7 points per serving (without brown rice)

Ingredient	Serving Size	Calories	Protein	Carbs	Fiber	Fat	GI	Points per Serving	Servings Used	Total Points
Olive Oil	1 tablespoon	120	0	0	0	14	-	1.2	1	1.2
Onion (chopped)	1 medium	64	1.5	15	2	0	-	0	1	0
Garlic (minced)	2 cloves	9	0.5	2	0.2	0	-	0	1	0
Spices (curry, cumin, coriander, turmeric)	-	~0	~0	~0	~0	~0	-	0	-	0
Diced Tomatoes (canned)	1 can (14.5 oz)	70	4	12	3	1	-	0	1	0
Vegetable Broth	1 cup	10	0.5	2	0	0	-	0	1	0
Eggplant (chopped)	1 cup	20	1	5	3	0	-	0	1	0
Zucchini (chopped)	1 cup	19	1	4	1	0.4	Low	0	1	0

Cauliflower Florets	1 cup	25	2	5	2	0	Low	0	1	0
Salt and Pepper	To taste	0	0	0	0	0	-	0	-	0
Fresh Cilantro	For garnish	~0	~0	~0	~0	~0	-	0	-	0
Brown Rice (cooked)	For serving (½ cup per serving)	216	4	44	3	2	Medium	2	-	-
Total		~643	~9.5	~87	~21.2	~17.4				1.2
Points per Serving (curry only)									4	0.3

Chapter 5: 42-Day No-Point Meal Plan

42-Day No-Point Mediterranean Meal Plan

Disclaimer:

- This meal plan is a sample and may need to be adjusted based on individual needs, preferences, and activity levels.
- Calorie counts are estimates and may vary depending on specific ingredients and portion sizes.
- It's always recommended to consult a healthcare professional or registered dietitian for personalized guidance on your weight loss journey.
- The estimated weight loss is a range and individual results may vary. Factors such as metabolism, activity level, and adherence to the plan will influence actual weight loss.

- **Calorie Target:** ~1500 calories per day
- **Expected Weight Loss:** 1-2 pounds

Day	Breakfast	Lunch/Light Bite	Dinner	Snacks (choose 2-3)
1	Mediterranean Oatmeal (pg 50)	Mediterranean Tuna Salad Lettuce Wraps (pg 87)	Baked Salmon with Mediterranean Salsa (pg 132)	Fruit and Yogurt Bowl (pg 78), Apple Slices with Almond Butter (pg 191)
2	Sunshine Scramble (pg 47)	Lemony Lentil Salad with Herbs (pg 90)	Chickpea and Vegetable Tagine (pg 135)	Greek Yogurt with Berries and Nuts (pg 182), Hard-Boiled Eggs (pg 197)
3	Greek Yogurt Parfait (pg 53)	Grilled Chicken & Veggie Skewers (pg 93)	Lentil Shepherd's Pie (pg 138)	Ants on a Log (pg 179), Fruit Salad (pg 201)
4	Savory Chickpea Scramble (pg 56)	Hummus & Veggie Pita Pockets (pg 96)	Mediterranean Grilled Chicken Salad (pg 141)	Cucumber Bites with Hummus (pg 187), Banana "Ice Cream" (pg 199)
5	Tuna Salad Stuffed Tomatoes (pg 59)	Caprese Salad (pg 99)	Shrimp Scampi with Zucchini Noodles (pg 144)	Homemade Trail Mix (pg 185), Hard-Boiled Eggs (pg 197)
6	Mediterranean Omelet (pg 62)	Black Bean & Corn Salad (pg 102)	Vegetable Paella (pg 147)	Fruit and Cheese Plate (pg 184), Apple Slices with Almond Butter (pg 191)

7	Lentil and Vegetable Curry (pg 65)	Mediterranean Quinoa Bowl (pg 105)	Mediterranean Baked Cod (pg 150)	Greek Yogurt with Berries and Nuts (pg 182), Roasted Chickpeas (pg 195)

Observations:

- You may experience increased energy levels due to the nutrient-dense foods
- Improved digestion and reduced bloating are likely as you increase fiber intake
- You may start to notice a decrease in cravings for unhealthy foods

- **Calorie Target:** ~1300 calories per day
- **Expected Weight Loss:** 1-2 pounds

Day	Breakfast	Lunch/Light Bite	Dinner	Snacks (choose 1-2)
1	Mediterranean Oatmeal (pg 50)	Lemony Lentil Salad with Herbs (pg 90)	Baked Salmon with Mediterranean Salsa (pg 132)	Fruit and Yogurt Bowl (pg 78)
2	Sunshine Scramble (pg 47)	Grilled Chicken & Veggie Skewers (pg 93)	Chickpea and Vegetable Tagine (pg 135)	Greek Yogurt with Berries and Nuts (pg 182)
3	Greek Yogurt Parfait (pg 53)	Hummus & Veggie Pita Pockets (pg 96)	Lentil Shepherd's Pie (pg 138)	Apple Slices with Almond Butter (pg 191)
4	Savory Chickpea Scramble (pg 56)	Caprese Salad (pg 99)	Mediterranean Grilled Chicken Salad (pg 141)	Hard-Boiled Eggs (pg 197)
5	Tuna Salad Stuffed Tomatoes (pg 59)	Black Bean & Corn Salad (pg 102)	Shrimp Scampi with Zucchini Noodles (pg 144)	Homemade Trail Mix (pg 185)
6	Mediterranean Omelet (pg 62)	Mediterranean Quinoa Bowl (pg 105)	Vegetable Paella (pg 147)	Fruit and Cheese Plate (pg 184)
7	Lentil and Vegetable Curry (pg 65)	Mediterranean Tuna Salad Lettuce Wraps (pg 87)	Mediterranean Baked Cod (pg 150)	Roasted Chickpeas (pg 195)

Observations:

- Continued improvement in energy levels and digestion.
- You may notice some initial weight loss and a decrease in clothing size.

- Your skin may start to look clearer and more radiant due to the increased intake of vitamins and antioxidants.

Suggestions for any relevant tests or assessments you may consider:

- Check your blood pressure and blood sugar levels again to monitor any changes

Recommendations:

- Continue to drink plenty of water throughout the day
- Increase your physical activity level gradually. Aim for at least 45 minutes of moderate-intensity exercise most days of the week.
- Pay attention to your hunger and fullness cues and adjust portion sizes as needed.

- **Calorie Target:** ~1100 calories per day
- **Expected Weight Loss:** 1-1.5 pounds

Day	Breakfast	Lunch/Light Bite	Dinner	Snacks (choose 1)
1	Mediterranean Oatmeal (pg 50)	Lemony Lentil Salad with Herbs (pg 90)	Baked Salmon with Mediterranean Salsa (pg 132)	Fruit and Yogurt Bowl (pg 78)
2	Sunshine Scramble (pg 47)	Grilled Chicken & Veggie Skewers (pg 93)	Lentil Shepherd's Pie (pg 138)	Greek Yogurt with Berries and Nuts (pg 182)
3	Greek Yogurt Parfait (pg 53)	Hummus & Veggie Pita Pockets (pg 96)	Mediterranean Grilled Chicken Salad (pg 141)	Apple Slices with Almond Butter (pg 191)
4	Savory Chickpea Scramble (pg 56)	Caprese Salad (pg 99)	Shrimp Scampi with Zucchini Noodles (pg 144)	Hard-Boiled Eggs (pg 197)
5	Tuna Salad Stuffed Tomatoes (pg 59)	Black Bean & Corn Salad (pg 102)	Vegetable Paella (pg 147)	Homemade Trail Mix (pg 185)
6	Mediterranean Omelet (pg 62)	Mediterranean Quinoa Bowl (pg 105)	Mediterranean Baked Cod (pg 150)	Fruit and Cheese Plate (pg 184)
7	Lentil and Vegetable Curry (pg 65)	Mediterranean Tuna Salad Lettuce Wraps (pg 87)	Stuffed Bell Peppers (pg 153)	Roasted Chickpeas (pg 195)

Observations:

- *You may experience continued weight loss and further improvements in energy levels and digestion.*
- *Your clothes may start to feel looser and more comfortable*
- *You may notice a decrease in cravings for unhealthy foods and a greater appreciation for the flavors of whole foods*

Suggestions for any relevant tests or assessments you may consider:

- *Consider getting a blood test to check your cholesterol levels and other health markers*

Week 4: Maintaining Momentum

- **Calorie Target:** ~900 calories per day
- **Expected Weight Loss:** 1-1.5 pounds

Day	Breakfast	Lunch/Light Bite	Dinner	Snacks (optional)
1	Mediterranean Oatmeal (pg 50)	Lemony Lentil Salad with Herbs (pg 90)	Baked Salmon with Mediterranean Salsa (pg 132)	Fruit Salad (pg 201)
2	Sunshine Scramble (pg 47)	Grilled Chicken & Veggie Skewers (pg 93)	Lentil Shepherd's Pie (pg 138)	-
3	Greek Yogurt Parfait (pg 53)	Hummus & Veggie Pita Pockets (pg 96)	Mediterranean Grilled Chicken Salad (pg 141)	-
4	Savory Chickpea Scramble (pg 56)	Caprese Salad (without cheese) (pg 99)	Shrimp Scampi with Zucchini Noodles (pg 144)	-
5	Tuna Salad Stuffed Tomatoes (pg 59)	Black Bean & Corn Salad (pg 102)	Vegetable Paella (pg 147)	-
6	Mediterranean Omelet (pg 62)	Mediterranean Quinoa Bowl (pg 105)	Mediterranean Baked Cod (pg 150)	-
7	Lentil and Vegetable Curry (pg 65)	Mediterranean Tuna Salad Lettuce Wraps (pg 87)	Stuffed Bell Peppers (pg 153)	-

Observations:

- Continued weight loss and improvements in overall health and well-being
- You may notice a significant difference in your body composition, with less body fat and more muscle definition
- You may feel more confident and empowered in your food choices

Suggestions for any relevant tests or assessments you may consider:

- Repeat the body composition analysis to track your progress

Recommendations:

- Continue to prioritize hydration and physical activity. Consider increasing the intensity or duration of your workouts
- Focus on mindful eating and listen to your body's hunger and fullness cues.
- Celebrate your progress and stay motivated!

Please note:

- As the calorie intake decreases, it's important to listen to your body and adjust portion sizes or add snacks as needed to ensure you're getting enough nutrients and energy to support your daily activities.
- Consult a healthcare professional or registered dietitian if you have any concerns or questions about your weight loss journey.

Chapter 6: Beyond the Plate

The Role of Exercise in Weight Loss

While the No-Point Mediterranean diet lays a strong foundation for healthy weight loss, incorporating regular physical activity is crucial for maximizing your results and achieving overall well-being. Exercise not only helps burn calories, but it also boosts metabolism, improves cardiovascular health, strengthens muscles and bones, and enhances mood and mental clarity. It's a vital component of a healthy lifestyle that complements the benefits of a nutritious diet.

Exercise Types and Recommendations

The beauty of exercise is its versatility. There are countless ways to get moving and find activities that you genuinely enjoy. Here are some exercise types that align well with the No-Point Mediterranean lifestyle:

Exercise Type	Description	Benefits	How to Incorporate
Walking	A low-impact, accessible activity that can be enjoyed by people of all fitness levels.	Improves cardiovascular health, strengthens muscles and bones, boosts mood, and aids in weight loss.	Aim for at least 30 minutes of brisk walking most days of the week. You can break it up into shorter intervals if needed.
Swimming	A full-body workout that is gentle on the joints.	Improves cardiovascular health, builds muscle strength and endurance, and is a great option for people	Aim for at least 30 minutes of swimming 2-3 times a week.

		with injuries or joint pain.	
Cycling	A fun and efficient way to get exercise, whether outdoors or on a stationary bike.	Improves cardiovascular health, strengthens leg muscles, and can be a great way to explore your surroundings.	Aim for at least 30 minutes of cycling 2-3 times a week.
Yoga	A mind-body practice that combines physical postures, breathing exercises, and meditation.	Improves flexibility, balance, strength, and reduces stress.	Practice yoga for at least 30 minutes 2-3 times a week. You can find beginner-friendly classes online or at your local gym or studio.
Strength Training	Exercises that use resistance to build muscle mass and strength.	Boosts metabolism, improves bone health, and helps sculpt and tone your body.	Aim for 2-3 strength training sessions per week, targeting all major muscle groups. You can use bodyweight exercises, free weights, or resistance bands.
Dancing	A fun and social way to get your heart rate up and burn calories.	Improves cardiovascular health, coordination, and balance.	Join a dance class, dance at home to your favorite music, or simply move your body to the rhythm whenever you can.
Hiking	A great way to enjoy nature while getting a full-body workout.	Improves cardiovascular health, strengthens muscles, and boosts mood.	Find trails near you and go for a hike on weekends or whenever you have free time.

Why Exercise is Essential

1. **Boosts Metabolism:** Regular exercise helps increase your metabolic rate, meaning you burn more calories even at rest. This can significantly contribute to your weight loss efforts.

2. **Improves Cardiovascular Health:** Exercise strengthens your heart and lungs, improving your overall cardiovascular fitness and reducing your risk of heart disease.

3. **Strengthens Muscles and Bones:** Weight-bearing exercises like walking, running, and strength training help build and maintain strong muscles and bones, which is crucial for overall health and mobility as you age

4. **Enhances Mood and Mental Clarity:** Exercise releases endorphins, which have mood-boosting effects. It can also help reduce stress and anxiety, contributing to a greater sense of well-being

Incorporating Exercise into Your Routine

- **Start Slowly and Gradually Increase:** If you're new to exercise, start with shorter, less intense workouts and gradually increase the duration and intensity as your fitness improves

- **Find Activities You Enjoy:** The key to sticking with an exercise routine is to find activities you genuinely enjoy. Experiment with different options until you find what works best for you

- **Make it a Habit:** Schedule regular exercise sessions into your calendar and treat them as important appointments

- **Find a Workout Buddy:** Exercising with a friend or family member can make it more enjoyable and help you stay motivated.

- **Listen to Your Body:** Pay attention to your body's signals and rest when needed. Don't push yourself too hard, especially when starting

Remember

Exercise is a journey, not a destination. It's about finding activities you enjoy, making them a part of your routine, and celebrating your progress along the way. By combining the No-Point Mediterranean diet with regular physical activity, you'll create a powerful synergy that supports your weight loss goals, improves your overall health, and enhances your quality of life.

Certainly, let's delve deeper into the remaining aspects of Chapter 6: Beyond the Plate, providing valuable insights and practical tips for long-term success.

Mindful Eating for Long-Term Success

Mindful eating is a powerful tool that can transform your relationship with food and support your weight loss journey in the long run. It involves paying full attention to the experience of eating, savoring each bite, and tuning into your body's hunger and fullness cues.

Key Principles of Mindful Eating:

> **Eat Slowly and Chew Thoroughly:** Take your time to enjoy each bite, chewing slowly and savoring the flavors and textures of your food. This allows your body to register fullness signals, preventing overeating.

> **Avoid Distractions:** When eating, avoid distractions like television, phones, or work. Focus on the present moment and the experience of eating.

> **Listen to Your Body:** Pay attention to your hunger and fullness cues. Eat when you're truly hungry and stop when you're comfortably full.

> **Appreciate Your Food:** Cultivate gratitude for the food you're eating, acknowledging the nourishment it provides and the effort that went into its creation.

Benefits of Mindful Eating:

1. **Improved Digestion:** By eating slowly and chewing thoroughly, you aid digestion and nutrient absorption
2. **Reduced Overeating:** Mindful eating helps you recognize fullness cues, preventing you from eating beyond your body's needs
3. **Enhanced Satisfaction:** By focusing on the present moment and savoring each bite, you'll derive greater enjoyment from your meals
4. **Healthier Food Choices:** Mindful eating encourages you to make conscious choices about the foods you eat, leading to a more balanced and nutritious diet
5. **Reduced Stress and Anxiety:** The practice of mindful eating can help calm your mind and reduce stress levels, promoting overall well-being

Navigating Social Situations and Dining Out

Social gatherings and dining out can pose challenges when trying to stick to a healthy eating plan. However, with a few mindful strategies, you can navigate these situations with confidence and still enjoy yourself

1. **Plan Ahead:** If you know you'll be dining out, check the restaurant's menu online beforehand and choose a dish that aligns with your dietary goals
2. **Don't Arrive Hungry:** Have a small, healthy snack before heading out to avoid overeating at the restaurant
3. **Make Mindful Choices:** Choose dishes that are grilled, baked, or steamed rather than fried
4. **Focus on Vegetables:** Order a side salad or extra vegetables to fill up on nutrient-dense foods
5. **Share or Take Leftovers Home:** If the portion sizes are large, consider sharing your meal with a friend or taking leftovers home for another meal
6. **Don't Feel Pressured:** It's okay to say no to foods that don't align with your goals. Politely explain your dietary preferences and focus on enjoying the company and conversation.

Tips for Staying Motivated and on Track

Maintaining motivation and staying on track with your weight loss journey can be challenging, but it's crucial for long-term success

- Set Realistic Goals: Start with small, achievable goals and gradually increase them as you progress.
- Track Your Progress :Keep a journal or use an app to track your food intake, exercise, and weight loss progress This can help you stay accountable and motivated
- Find a Support System: Surround yourself with supportive friends, family, or a weight loss group to encourage and motivate you along the way
- Celebrate Your Successes: Acknowledge your achievements, no matter how small. Celebrate milestones and reward yourself for your hard work
- Don't Give Up: There will be setbacks and challenges along the way. Don't get discouraged; pick yourself up and keep moving forward

By incorporating mindful eating practices, navigating social situations with confidence, and staying motivated, you'll set yourself up for long-term success on your No-Point Mediterranean journey. Remember, it's about progress, not perfection. Embrace the process, enjoy the delicious and nutritious foods, and celebrate every step towards a healthier, happier you!

Conclusion

Embracing a Sustainable Lifestyle

As you reach the end of this cookbook, I hope you've gained a deeper understanding of the No-Point Mediterranean approach and its transformative power. Remember, this is not just a 42-day meal plan; it's a blueprint for a sustainable lifestyle that nourishes your body, mind, and soul.

By prioritizing whole, unprocessed foods, savoring each bite, and incorporating regular physical activity, you've embarked on a journey that goes far beyond weight loss. You've cultivated a healthier relationship with food, learned to listen to your body's signals, and embraced a more mindful approach to eating.

Celebrating Your Achievements

Take a moment to reflect on your journey and celebrate your achievements, both big and small. Whether you've reached your weight loss goal, improved your energy levels, or simply feel more confident and empowered in your choices, each step forward is a victory worth celebrating.

Remember, the No-Point Mediterranean lifestyle is not about perfection; it's about progress. It's about making choices that support your health and well-being, one meal at a time. Be proud of the changes you've made and the commitment you've shown to yourself.

Your Ongoing Journey to Wellness

This cookbook is just the beginning of your journey to wellness. As you continue to embrace the No-Point Mediterranean lifestyle, you'll discover new recipes, explore different flavors, and find creative ways to nourish your body.

Remember, this is a lifelong journey, not a destination. There will be challenges along the way, but with the tools and knowledge you've gained, you're well-equipped to navigate them with grace and resilience.

We'd Love to Hear from You!

I'm excited to see the positive transformations you'll experience as you embrace the No-Point Mediterranean lifestyle. Please share your successes, challenges, and feedback with us on Amazon or your favourite Bookstore. Your journey can inspire others and create a ripple effect of health and well-being.

Remember, you are not alone on this journey. We're here to support you every step of the way.

To your continued health and happiness!

Angelina

Made in the USA
Monee, IL
13 October 2024

67745728R10144